Are You Getting Screwed On Your Property Taxes?

How To Find Out and How To Fix It!

by Patricia Quintilian, Esq.

Published by Lightbearers Publishing
Copyright 2010 Patricia Quintilian, Esq.
ISBN: 978-0-9829334-0-4

"The tax revolts and tea parties of 2009 signaled the beginning of the Second American Revolution. A Coalition of the Cash Strapped is ready to fight, and ***Are You Getting Screwed on your Property Taxes? How To Find Out & How To Fix It!*** is the practical guide to help unite and prepare them for battle."

—*Gerald Celente, Founder & Director, The Trends Institute*

Are You Getting Screwed On Your Property Taxes?

How To Find Out and How To Fix It!

Chapter One
Why You Need This Book

What is the difference between a taxidermist and a tax assessor?
A taxidermist takes only your skin. ~ Mark Twain

If you asked me several years ago if I needed a book like this, I would have said, "of course not!" Only when I was slapped with excessive and vindictive property taxes and personally targeted for exercising my legal rights did I begin my search for a book to help me navigate my way through my property tax nightmare. I found none! In fact, there was no practical information anywhere that would help me with my horrible five year battle with my town's assessors.

After all, who knew that assessors could decrease their own property values by tens of thousands of dollars under market value and never get caught? Who knew that when assessors break the law or put incorrect numbers on a taxpayer's property record card, there is no accountability and no state agency to prosecute them? Who knew that you would be forced to fight the same battle year after year at the Appellate Tax Board because the assessors just didn't like you or wanted to get even with you for contesting your property taxes? Who knew that you would have to pay for an appraiser, a lawyer, take time off from work, and appear in court to plead your case while the assessors sat on their derrieres and didn't even have to show up? I uncovered all of this shocking information and much more.

The good news is that I managed to accomplish something unusual and actually won my property tax battles and you will benefit greatly from my experience. The laws in Massachusetts and most other states are truly stacked against the homeowner and firmly skewed in favor of the assessors and the state. Because of this inherent favoritism written into the law, you must be well informed on this entire subject in order to win your case.

This book will get you that information quickly and efficiently. I will show you how to:

- get a copy of your property record card;
- how to understand it;
- how to use various appraisal methods to your advantage;
- compare your property record card to your neighbors and assessors;
- challenge your home's value at every level, from your local assessor's office to the courtroom;
- represent yourself in a courtroom; and,
- determine whether your lawyer, if you hired one, is doing a good job.

You may be shocked and appalled at the level of corruption that has permeated a dysfunctional and complicated property tax system. Many homeowners, while fighting their own property tax battles, independently uncovered a system so corrupt and so unchecked that it left all of us stunned. This corruption not only adversely affected us, but many other unsuspecting property owners as well. YOU are probably one of them.

When you read this book and look into your own property tax situation, you will more than likely discover that you are getting screwed on your property taxes and have been for years. Most homeowners have never seen their property record cards because their mortgage companies usually pay their property taxes. Even if you have seen your property record card, you probably will not understand it. Yet the key to determining how the assessors decide your property tax fate is within the four corners of your property record card. As such, you better learn how to read the darn thing.

Once you are educated in the art of property record card translation, you will want to check yours thoroughly. Why? The answer is simple. With so little training required of assessors in some states and the lack of any meaningful assessor oversight, it is unlikely that they came up with the correct assessment. They may not even know how to measure your house correctly. Keep in mind that your value is largely based on measurements and hard data such as the number of bedrooms, bathrooms, square footage, etc., and one more thing – the complete discretion of the assessors. Yes, the assessors can determine what your property is worth based on nothing more than their OPINION. They can even decide what they want your home to be worth first and then make up numbers to support their decision. Yes, we've seen it done that way! They can also decide to place imaginary buildings on your property and then tax you on them. If you do not check your property record card, you will pay for every one of their "errors" and if you miss your window of opportunity to file for an abatement (a decrease in your assessment), you will find that you have no recourse at all to fix their "mistakes."

All of this information may send you screaming into the night. Our economy is in a state of disarray and politicians have run up more debt than ever before. Against this backdrop, taxing authorities are looking to fill their ever-decreasing coffers. Assessors are relying on your ignorance of the system and present inability to contest your property tax bills as a means to increase revenue. Recent statistics indicate that 60% or more of property owners are being overassessed, but only 2% are applying for abatements and filing appeals! Meanwhile, if you blindly trust your assessors to be fair, you may find your trust is misplaced. Real estate values are going DOWN, but your tax bill is mysteriously going UP. Hmmmmm.

Although you are about to read some incredibly horrific trials and tribulations of property owners who fought against assessor negligence and corruption, this is not an indictment of all assessors or the Department of Revenue in every state. Rather, these events call attention to a property tax system that is systemically flawed and designed with insufficient fail-safe mechanisms. By design, the system collects property taxes in an unequal and unfair manner.

Although this book describes in great detail the problematic state of property tax affairs in Massachusetts, this information is not just for Massachusetts' residents. The suggestions in this book will help you no matter where you live and own property. This book is for:
- People who currently own property;
- People about to purchase a home. If you can't afford the taxes now or in the future, your new home will be seized by the government;
- People filing for abatements;
- People involved in the legal process fighting for an abatement;

- People involved in the legal process who already have a lawyer and want to make sure his or her lawyer is doing everything possible to win the case;
- Elected officials across the country who must become informed regarding property taxation;
- Assessors and appraisers working in the field;
- Attorneys who are representing homeowners in property tax litigation.

All across this country, property tax systems are confusing, difficult to understand, and rigged on the side of the assessors. All too often, assessors are not held accountable for their mistakes. I wrote this book to bring these unfair practices to the light of day. Not only will this book give you a fighting chance in court, but it will give you an opportunity to organize with like-minded property owners and change the property tax system. Some taxpayers have already taken a stand to abolish property taxes altogether in their states. We, as property owners, must take a stand and embrace an American revolution in property taxation. It is time for politicians to head our cry for "fairness" in taxation and end our suffering from burdensome property taxes. It is time to demand our RIGHT to own our homes without endless taxation. After reading this book, you will be ready, forewarned and effectively armed with the information you need to mobilize, exchange ideas, and fight unfair taxation both in and out of court!

Chapter Two
My Nightmare—Why I Wrote This Book

*Nearly all men can stand adversity, but if you want to test
a man's character, give him power. ~ Abraham Lincoln*

I began my odyssey into property tax hell when I built a geodesic dome[1] in a small New England town. The obtainment of my Certificate of Occupancy[2] for my eco-friendly home was cause for celebration, or so I thought. Within months, this celebratory occupancy was marred by the town's assessors overassessing my home for five long years. Thus began my tortuous journey into property tax hell.

The assessors initially assessed my home $62,500 above the actual cost to build the structure. In addition, my property record card contained many blatant errors. A property record card is a document created by your assessor with information concerning how your assessor arrived at your assessment. I was the general contractor for my home so I knew exactly, to the penny, how much it cost to build it. How fair is it to pay property taxes on a home that is $62,500 above the building cost? I quickly found out that the property tax system is not fair.

[1] A ten-sided eco-friendly home designed by Buckminster Fuller.
[2] Legal permission to move into my home.

Moreover, other geodesic homes in the area were assessed at much lower assessments than mine, a great cause for concern. I contacted the assessors in a futile attempt to find out why my home was assessed so high compared to other geodesic homes and why my assessment was $62,500 above the actual building cost.

I immediately told the assessors that there were numerous mistakes made on my property record card. One of the mistakes concerned the square footage of my home, a factor that affects market value. After three trips to my property and many, many measurements, the assessors' final square footage for the first and second floor were identical, an obvious error. Logically, would a dome be a dome if the two floors had the same square footage? The answer is clearly "no." Such mistakes were obviously the product of the assessors' ignorance and inexperience dealing with such an unusual ten sided structure. Surely, a meeting would fix such glaring errors. To my dismay, these errors were never corrected until all of the assessors resigned and were replaced by new ones five years later. I was, and still am, horrified at this protracted ineptitude.

The initial meeting with the assessors took place in my dome and it began with an ominous tone. One assessor immediately explained that the town's assessments were based upon "square footage." Shocked, I asked, "Isn't it based upon market value?" "Oh no," replied the assessor assertively. This comment is simply wrong since the law requires that taxes be assessed at the "fair cash value" of your home. This is something that an assessor should know.

Venturing further, I then asked, "what about the two floors having the same square footage?" The assessor replied, "So?" It eventually took a structural engineer hired by me at a cost of $1,500 to explain to the assessors that a dome's top floor will necessarily have less square footage than the bottom floor or it would not be a dome. At one point, the assessors wanted to settle the square footage issue and split the difference between my expert's square footage calculation and the assessors' guess. I told the assessors that square footage has an exact number and it would violate the laws of physics to negotiate and compromise an immutable characteristic such as square footage. They still refused to acknowledge their errors. For the next five years, I paid taxes on part of my second floor that simply did not exist. Again, I was horrified. Adding insult to injury, I was also assessed on a front porch that did not exist. This meeting ended unsuccessfully and the nightmare grew exponentially.

In an attempt to fix these errors, I filed an abatement with my assessors, and it was denied. Not surprising. I then petitioned the Appellate Tax Board.[3] The Appellate Tax Board reduced the assessment considerably and the issue appeared resolved. This was a short-lived victory however. The assessors exacted their revenge by raising my assessment the following year by $114,000, an increase of 47%. There were no increases in the town for any property that were even close to my assessment's increase. Even more disturbing was that my home was now the third highest assessed property in the entire town for that year. According to my assessment, I was now grouped in the same category as five and six bedroom homes. I have a modest three bedroom home with approximately 2,000 square feet of living space, but I was forced to pay higher taxes commensurate with the larger and more expensive homes in town. It was clear that this outrageous increase was because I dared to challenge their assessment. The assessors were abusing their power.

[3] The Appellate Tax Board is a quasi-judicial state agency that handles appeals of state and local taxes.

I filed an abatement for a second year, it was denied. I petitioned the Appellate Tax Board and the assessment was again reduced. However, at the hearing, the assessors argued and submitted my property record card with an assessment of $274,700 as the fair cash value of my home. Bear in mind that the Appellate Tax Board's ruling was that my home was valued at $241,600 for the prior year. Eight months later, I was billed for an assessment of $355,600. I now had two property record cards issued for the same fiscal tax year with very different assessments with no improvements added to my home. In eight months, my assessment increased $80,900, an increase of 29% using their assessments. It would have been an even greater increase using the ATB's assessed value of my home. There should only be one property record card issued for each tax year. How does one explain two property record cards issued for the same tax year with very different assessments? There is simply no rational explanation for two property record cards issued for the same year with such a disparity in assessments. The only logical explanation is that this was "payback" and designed to deter me from exercising my rights under the law.

This same scenario played out for the next three years. My assessments were increased for no apparent reason, abatements were filed with no success and the Appellate Tax Board was repeatedly petitioned. I continually asked for help with these clearly vindictive assessments at the Appellate Tax Board and was told by the commissioner that the only issue he was interested in was the fair cash value of my home for the contested fiscal year and nothing more. All of the irregularities and improper conduct of the assessors that I uncovered fell on deaf ears.

Year after year, I had to prepare and petition the Appellate Tax

Board. The assessors were singling me out because I dared to question their practices. The assessors would routinely tell me that the information that I requested was too burdensome for them to retrieve. I was told that the computer broke or that they were using a new computer system that prevented them from retrieving information from previous years. I was routinely told that the assessors did not come up with the figures, but that "the computer did it." I was stonewalled at every turn.

Not only was filing with the Appellate Tax Board for five consecutive years in and of itself ridiculous, but this unnecessary legal wrangling interfered with my normal workload. The burden of fighting the assessors was even reaching closer to home. During this time period, I would find empty beer cans placed conspicuously and strategically on my property so that I would know that someone had trespassed in order to send me a message. Even more treacherous, nails were thrown at the end of my driveway that resulted in many flat tires. I became concerned for my safety. Another, more serious tactic was needed in order to get these issues resolved.

I wrote the Department of Revenue's commissioner, the head of an agency that allegedly handles the oversight of assessors in the state of Massachusetts. This agency has been remiss in supervising town assessors and its lack of oversight has enabled town assessors to unfairly and arbitrarily assess homes with impunity. However, the only reason this letter proved fruitful in my case was because I am a lawyer and I submitted my letter with a petition of approximately ninety signatures from town residents requesting an investigation into the town's assessment practices. Further, the outrageous conduct of the assessors was now attracting media attention. The local newspapers were investigating the unfairness and irregularities in the town's assessment practices. The light of day was now shining on the assessors' improper practices and the Department of Revenue's failure to regulate local assessments. Something had to be done.

This declaration of taxpayer outrage concerning the town's unfair property taxation spread rapidly and more corruption was revealed. One assessor's property tax assessment for his home (building and land) only increased by a total of $2,000 for a ten year period that also included the height of the real estate boom. In retort, this assessor told the media that he did nothing wrong. The state agency was also listening. Finally, the agency withdrew the town's certification; this meant that taxes could no longer be collected by the town. Within six months, all of the assessors resigned or did not seek re-election.

It took five long years of legal and political maneuvering to unseat the corrupt and incompetent assessors who ruled without any oversight or accountability. Finally, my problem was solved and I have not filed an abatement or petitioned the Appellate Tax Board since the assessors' replacement.

Looking at this closely, anyone can see that the system is built for corruption. There is no oversight, no accountability and the laws do not deter bad behavior on the part of assessors. The solution to my problem will live only as long as the present assessors, who have their own moral compasses, remain in office. The dark forces of greed and evil can resurface just as quickly if new assessors without any sense of fair play replace these honorable ones. Is it fair and intelligent to play Russian roulette with property tax assessments and depend on the integrity of each individual assessor? Or, shouldn't the system be built to prevent these kinds of abuses?

During my odyssey into property tax hell, I met many other tortured souls along the way. Many people told me their horror stories and requested my help. The injustice underlying all of their stories, as well as my own, propelled me to write this book. The single force driving my tenacity in not allowing the assessors to continue their unfair and discriminatory practices was the impact their disparate taxation had on the fixed income homeowners that I met. These homeowners were noticeably afraid of any more tax increases and of drawing the wrath of the assessors. Several taxpayers were told, "If they file for an abatement, then somebody else would have to pay their share of taxes." This intimidation had been going on for a very, very long time. When I raised the issue to a Department of Revenue employee, she acknowledged that they "have had problems with these assessors before." They knew of the problems and did nothing.

The defining moment that spurred me into action was when I was in one of my five hearings and the assessor told the commissioner that I refused to let the assessors on my property to do the proper measurements. This was particularly egregious because the assessors had been on my property three times that fiscal year and there was no way this could be attributed to a mistake. This was an outright lie. As an honest person with a very high sense of "right and wrong," this conduct crossed the line for me and I decided right then and there to do whatever was necessary to see that justice was done. At great personal and financial cost to me, I spent the ensuing years in pursuit of that goal and this book was written to help other people who are experiencing the same unfair and punitive taxation that I experienced.

If I experienced so many problems as an attorney who is trained to maneuver through the legal system, I can only imagine what it is like for those who have no experience in this area. Although it is highly touted that people can represent themselves, most people cannot afford to take the time off from their daily jobs to become informed and fight unfair taxation by themselves, nor can they afford legal representation. It is my desire to help the average homeowner effectively maneuver through this frustrating maze of nonsense.

17

Chapter Three
Lessons From the Past—
Property Tax History

You can have a Lord, you can have a King, but the man
to fear is the tax assessor. ~ Anonymous citizen of Lasgash

Why examine the history of property taxes? The answer is simple. There is much to learn from the successes and failures of preceding property tax systems. Today, there is tremendous political discord in our society and the relentless burden of increasing taxes only adds to this dissonance. Rising taxes hang over our heads like the sword of Damocles. Any potential to ward off this sword rests in examining the successes and pitfalls of prior property tax systems. Succinctly stated by Winston Churchill, "Those that fail to learn from history are doomed to repeat it."

Imagine getting hit in the head with your property tax bill. Although you may feel like you're getting hit in the head with your tax bill every year, people in the ancient city-state of Lagash, now known as Iraq, actually could get hit in the head with their tax bills. They, in fact, received their property tax bills on clay tablets. Thus began the first property tax system in recorded history. Although most people think that property taxes are a recent invention of the modern era, the clay tablets were sent to the residents of Lagash thousands of years ago in six thousand B.C. Property taxes then spread like a virus throughout the ancient world of Egypt, Babylon, Persia and China.

World conqueror, Alexander the Great (356 B.C. – 323B.C.) was a military genius who used taxes to expand his empire. After conquering many lands, he left administrators in charge of his territories with explicit instructions on how to collect property taxes. He was smarter than his kingly predecessor who taxed his subjects to the hilt and gave them no benefits in return. In contrast, Alexander slashed taxes in half and used the money to improve his subjects' living conditions. The conquered actually paid fewer taxes and received more benefits. Since Alexander's subjects were getting something of value for paying their taxes, they were less inclined to revolt against Alexander's administrators. A lesson our present politicians should heed. Where is a smart ruler like Alexander when you need one?

Moving along the historical time line, between 200 B.C. to 300 A.D., the Romans, further expanding the taxing frenzy, began taxing not only their subjects' land, but also their buildings, livestock, trees, vines and personal property. These taxes were then used to fund Roman wars. For example, when Julius Caesar prepared for the Gaulic campaign and discovered that there was not enough money to fund the war, his battle cry was, "Send out the assessors!" Sound familiar? When Caesar was questioned about why he was occupying himself with something as trivial as taxes, he reportedly replied, "My friend, taxes are the chief business of a conqueror of the world." A mantra that has transcended time.

Where Alexander the Great gave his subjects a good return on their taxes by way of services, Caesar's greed to tax more and provide less was the beginning of the end of the Roman Empire. Tiberius Caesar cut back on public improvements and retained huge portions of collected taxes in his treasury. This precipitated a financial crisis where money was in short supply. The tax rates soared. The wealthy Senate class was taxed so severely that their properties were often confiscated or they were driven from their land. Emperors began reducing the silver content of coins, which ultimately undermined public confidence in their currency. This incredibly shortsighted move completely destroyed the economy. In fact, some small landowners were forced into bankruptcy by the heavy burden of taxation. In order to escape this burden, these landowners opted to become slaves of the larger landowners until it was declared illegal by Emperor Valens (368 A.D.). Eventually, the entire system broke down. There was no longer a monetary system and everyone went back to bartering. With no ability to pay an army, barbarians invaded Rome. However, many citizens were happier to be conquered by barbarians because they were finally freed of the excessive tax burdens imposed by Roman rulers. Assessors eventually lost their positions of honor and were now looked upon as evil people who often required military escort to prevent them from being murdered.

In feudal England, the lords and kings owned the land, but most peasants paid taxes referred to as "rent" for each year. If the land was especially productive, the rental value was increased. Perhaps we should really call our property taxes "rent" as they did in feudal times. Are we not really renting our properties from the government? Between the tenth and twelfth centuries, an average peasant paid one tenth (a tithe) of the value of crops to the lord who then passed on a certain percentage to the king. Peasants were also required to give an additional one tenth of their crops to the church.

Stories of heavy taxation also crept into folklore. Lady Godiva was an historical figure who also fought unfair taxation. According to legend, Leofric, the Anglo-Saxon earl of Mercia, imposed heavy taxes on his subjects. Lady Godiva protested these taxes by riding nude on a white horse through the town of Coventry after first requesting that all citizens should stay inside during her ride. Legend has it that an abatement (a reduction in taxes) was given. True or fanciful, this creative way to get one's property taxes reduced is best not attempted in today's world. Not only would you fail to get an abatement, you would probably end up with a police escort to your local jail.

In 1066, William the Conqueror crafted his own form of land taxation. Town officials were required to keep records of everyone who owned property. "Big Brother" started way before George Orwell's *1984*. Each town kept a book of assessments for each property and the property tax owed by each owner. Each parcel was measured and its value estimated. This book was called the *Doomsday Book*, and the name lasted for hundreds of years. Some people in England still refer to assessor's records as the Doomsday book even to this day. How apropos.

In 1215, England's King John was clearly out of control and abusing his power when he raised taxes to a confiscatory level. He was eventually forced to sign the Magna Carta, which limited a king's power to raise revenue. After the historic signing, taxes could only be collected with the consent of his barons. Following this policy, in 1689, the English Bill of Rights prohibited a king from taxing the populace without Parliament's consent. By the sixteenth century, the king's own lands and estates were being taxed – a small measure of equity that should have been implemented from the beginning!

Around 1290, the imposition of personal property taxes began in England with exemptions for the poorest and the church. Certain items such as a knight's armor and a merchant's capital were also not taxed. The personal property tax rate was one tenth for those who resided in the cities and one fifteenth for rural residents. These assessments were rough estimates of a person's assets and contrary to today, underassessment was the norm. The average tax equaled about two shillings per year or about two days wages for a peasant. People began moving assets to avoid taxes and many learned to hide their personal property. The wealthier taxpayers who had multiple residences moved assets from one residence to another to avoid taxation.

The genesis of America's property tax system began in 1662. Between 1662 and 1689, a hearth tax was administered in England. A modern day precursor, this tax was an estimate of a building's value. Assessors recorded the number and size of hearths in each home and determined value accordingly. A one-hearth house received a low assessment compared to some mansions that had twenty or thirty heated rooms. This tax was so hated that it was eventually phased out! Perhaps a solution to the problems of our present day property tax system?

When the Pilgrims crossed the Atlantic and landed in Plymouth, Massachusetts, they allegedly received a bundle of arrows wrapped in snakeskin. The Pilgrims interpreted this as a threat from the local Indians. As a result, they decided to build a fort. The 102 Pilgrims formed a pact that bound them to a set of laws, among them the creation of taxes and assessments. Bad move. People were generally allocated equal portions of land, but the more productive land was assessed at a higher rate. The Pilgrim Puritans collected property taxes to pay for the church and the religious education of their children. It was mandatory that everyone pay the property tax regardless of one's religion. Taxes from Boston's towns went directly to the church. This practice lasted for over one hundred years.

There is some historical evidence of compassion directed towards people who were too sick, elderly or poor to pay taxes. Some taxpayers were granted exemptions and even received a certain amount of money from a general tax fund. You certainly won't find that level of compassion today. I have heard many accounts of the elderly being taken advantage of by assessors who overvalued their properties and were confident that the elderly would not contest their assessments. During the time period of the Pilgrim-Puritans, there were complaints of inequitable assessments, abatement irregularities, and residency fraud (i.e., moving assets to another town when the assessors were coming). So, yes, even back then, taxpayers were unhappy with inequality!

Shortly after the Revolutionary War, the new congress instituted a national property tax based upon the number and size of a house's windows and doors. A tax rebellion was spearheaded by John Fries, a veteran of the Revolutionary War. The sight of assessors riding through the countryside counting windows evoked strong community opposition. These assessors were captured, threatened and many resigned as a result. Many of the residents of Pennsylvania refused to pay the tax. John Fries and his compatriots were subsequently arrested, tried and convicted of treason. For his efforts, Fries was sentenced to death. John Adams later pardoned this war veteran and the tax was eventually repealed.

After the revolution, there were two main groups of thought: One group followed Alexander Hamilton's belief that there should be a larger, central government with greater revenue raising capability than the states. The second group followed Thomas Jefferson's philosophy that revenue should be raised locally because it is more democratic. Historically, Jefferson was very leery of big government becoming a tyrannical institution. Hamilton also argued that the country should push for industrial development, while Jefferson pushed for a more agrarian society. Alexander Hamilton was the first United States Secretary of the Treasury and credited with helping create the foundation for a capitalist system. Historically, Hamilton's federalist point of view eventually won out.

Unbeknownst to most people, Abraham Lincoln handled property tax cases in the Illinois courts. He handled three famous cases whose property tax issues are still litigated today. Lincoln's cases that obtained a measure of notoriety in property tax law are as follow:

1. The owner of a ferryboat moved his boat out of its assessing jurisdiction on the lien date. The assessor taxed the boat at a normal assessment and Lincoln appealed the case arguing that the boat was not in the assessor's jurisdiction on the lien date. He won the case.

2. Another case involved a valuation issue for the Illinois Central Railroad. The railroad was under construction and approximately half complete on the lien date. Lincoln contended that the property was assessed as though the work was completed, but the assessment should have reflected its true value as half

constructed. He won this case for the biggest legal fee of his life, $5,000.

3. He tried another railroad case on an exemption issue and won that case as well.

In the ensuing years, taxation in the United States became more complex and less transparent. Throughout the nineteenth century, most state and local governments raised their revenue through property taxes. However, the South predominantly raised its revenues through "poll taxes," a system of taxation where a certain amount was charged depending on the rental value of a house with a flat rate paid by every adult, thus earning the nickname "Poll Tax." This is different from the latter poll tax used in the South to deter blacks from registering to vote. The value of the charge was set by the local authority and was intended to fund each local council's infrastructure and needed community services. This Poll Tax was eventually phased out.

During the Great Depression, incomes dropped right along with decreasing property tax revenue. The depression sparked a national fiscal reform movement where many states began collecting sales taxes while cutting property taxes. Additionally, sixteen states also implemented property tax limitation laws. These reform groups advocated for lower taxes, reduced penalties for delinquent taxes, and lower governmental spending. Not a bad solution for our present day fiscal crises. Eventually, these groups disbanded when Prohibition ended and alcohol taxes were collected. In 1934, the government collected $259 million in alcohol tax revenue and in 1939, $624 million.

This additional tax revenue eased the burden on taxpayers by lessening the need for property tax revenue.

Although these tax reform groups disbanded, they did affect some major tax reforms in the first half of the twentieth century. Personal property taxes were narrowly defined and there was almost a complete elimination of intangible property taxation. Exemptions were created for the sick, elderly, poor, and farm owners. Homestead exemptions were created. There were limits placed on the percentage of one's income going to property taxes. Some states even instituted property tax limits.

During the 1970's, states that had not implemented property tax limits came under increasing pressure to reform their property tax systems. For example, on June 7, 1978, Proposition 13 passed in California, which limited property assessments to their current value plus a 2% increase for every year thereafter. When the property sold or was newly constructed, the assessment process began with the new sale's price and the ensuing yearly 2% limitation.

In Massachusetts, after multiple years of taxpayer complaints and failed attempts to lower property taxes, on November 4, 1978, Proposition 2½ passed, which severely limited the amount and growth of property taxes. Despite this proposition, property taxes are growing at an alarming rate. To compound this problem, the present day property tax system is a nightmare. It is both difficult to navigate and unfair to the property owner.

The most recent and volatile tax revolt occurred in England in 1990 and it eventually forced Prime Minister Margaret Thatcher to resign from office. The conservative government, led by Prime Minister Thatcher, introduced a tax called the "Community Charge," also known as the "poll tax." The poll tax was a fixed tax per head that was the same for everyone. As a result of this tax, mass demonstrations were held with some developing into mass riots. By far, the largest and most notorious riot occurred in central London on March 31, 1990, shortly before the poll tax was to be implemented. Prime Minister Margaret Thatcher resigned the same year and her successor abolished this unpopular tax. The poll tax was replaced with a "Council Tax," a tax system based upon property's market value with a discount for people living alone. This tax revolt was successful and strong enough to bring down the reigning political party. History teaches us that when many speak as one voice, the world can be changed.

Since that fateful day in Iraq, most of the ensuing property tax systems have been corrupt and unfair. The key to successful property taxation is to keep taxes simple, low, and offer taxpayers real value for the taxes they pay. Such is the lesson Alexander the Great taught more than two thousand years ago. This lesson has long been forgotten as we face complicated systems with little or no transparency and unending increases in property taxes with little or no benefits to the taxpayer. Having failed to learn the lessons of history, will we be doomed to follow the fate of the Roman Empire?

Chapter Four
Horror Stories From the
Property Tax Trenches

Man made the city, God made the country...
and the devil made the small town.

You will probably find this chapter the most entertaining. It may make you laugh or cry, sometimes both at the same time. This chapter was the hardest to write because I personally felt the heartbreak, frustration and helplessness of each taxpayer who shared his or her story of victimization. All of these stories are true. The names and identifying characteristics have been changed to protect the property owners who have expressed their fears of further harassment. This is NOT an indictment of all assessors. Some assessors are fair, honorable, and competent. Unfortunately, these assessors did not work in these towns...

An owner of 130 acres of forestland had to reach for his heart pills when he saw that his property tax bill for 2010, in a very down market, had increased 520%. He discovered that all of the town's residents did not have any tax increases, but all of the non-residents had enormous tax increases. This type of disparate taxation is very common in small towns. This discriminated group got together to fight these unfair assessments and filed for abatements. The assessors denied all of them. Exasperated, a member of this group consulted his attorney and was advised not to appeal his case at the ATB because it would be too costly. This property owner did not have the benefit of this book and did not even consider presenting his case to the ATB without the services of an attorney. On advice of counsel, he decided not to appeal his case and is now stuck with an egregious and ridiculous property tax bill. This is what some assessors count on when they abuse their power; the common mistaken belief that the process is too expensive or time-consuming to take them on.

In another town, a couple questioned an unusually high valuation on their vacant piece of land that fell into the category of an "unbuildable lot" due to its small size (under an acre). When they questioned their assessor about the high value, she said she would look into it. When the couple received their adjusted tax bill, they discovered that rather than a reduction in the assessed value, the assessor doubled the value of their lot. I guess their assessor didn't take kindly to being questioned. The following year, in order to ensure this couple got the message, the assessor again doubled the assessed value of their lot, which now made the assessed value four times the initial value they questioned. This story is not unusual and far too often, taxpayers live in fear of their assessors. It is quite apparent why the taxpayers, who were kind enough to share their stories with me, asked to have their identities hidden.

Even attorneys are targeted in this dubious system. An attorney in New York uncovered corruption in the assessor's office and filed a lawsuit to address the problems. This lawyer and her family were targeted and threatened physical harm if she continued her fight. Fearing for her family's safety, she moved to another state. Eroding legal protection for whistleblowers is a tragedy and the legal system has failed those of us who are working for honesty and accountability in our government.

Vicki is another example of a property owner who tried to do "the right thing." When she became aware of problems in her town's assessors' office, she decided to become an assessor and help get things straightened out. Vicki was somewhat unusual because she actually had a background in real estate and accounting. What she walked into, however, was a maelstrom of "mismanagement" that had been in place for years and wasn't about to change.

One of the first things Vicki did was to check her property record card. To her dismay, she discovered that she had been taxed for five years on a building that didn't exist. Yes, you read that right. She was taxed on a building that was not now, or in the past, ever on her property. When she brought this blatant error to the attention of the other assessors, they said that they would come to her property and "see for themselves." When they arrived at Vicki's home and could not find the building, the chair of the Assessor board turned to her and asked, "What did you do with it?" Vicki, aghast at their question, told them that there never was a building on her property and that they had made a ridiculous entry on her property record card for years, which resulted in her paying $10,000 more than she should have! The assessors gave Vicki an abatement for the invisible building for only one year because there was a time limitation on abatements. To add insult to injury, these assessors told Vicki that it was her responsibility to check the entries on her record card and since she hadn't checked them, it was just too bad for her. Let's blame the homeowner for assessor mistakes. This is as nonsensical as the often stated assessor excuse that "the computer did it."

This assessor malfeasance spurred Vicki to check all the property record cards in her town and what she found frizzed her already beautifully curled hair. She found a problem with almost every single property record card. Violations of Department of Revenue guidelines and blatant violations of the law, disparate assessments, strange neighborhood assignments that increased certain residents' assessments, false land assignments, and current and former assessors' homes valued way below market value. As Vicki poured through the cards, one property record card stood out more than the others, a record card for the current assessor who had also been an assessor in the past. This assessor had a newly renovated 3 bedroom house, post and beam construction, a state of the art kitchen with radiant floor heating and her home was valued at $33,500. Her land had a forestry designation, but the land value was much lower than the tables allowed. Vicki thought to herself, "this is just plain wrong and unfair to everyone else in town."

With evidence in hand, Vicki approached the DOR. "They couldn't have cared less," she exclaimed. She showed a DOR representative the multiple violations of the law on the record cards and escorted him personally to the house owned by the assessor in question. The assessor's house also had an eleven hundred square foot addition that was not reported on the property record card. The DOR representative just shrugged his shoulders and said, "I can't do anything about that!" Things went from bad to worse when Vicki tried to make the appropriate changes in the assessors' office. She was told point blank by the other assessors that "this is how things are done here and stop trying to rock the boat." Eventually, Vicki, with all her good intentions to make things fair for all the property owners in her town, was driven out of office. Another example of unregulated governmental abuse of power.

In another town, Jeff went to pay his assessor a visit in her office to question his abnormally high valuation; his tax bill increased by $2,000 in one year. While there, he saw his assessor's property record card on the desk. Angered by what he saw, Jeff heatedly protested to this assessor, "You are paying less taxes on your 4 bedroom house than me on my 2 bedroom camp with no electricity, no plumbing, on a dirt road in a town with no goddamn services." Nothing was done by this assessor to address Jeff's concerns. To this day, and still angered by the situation, Jeff further explained that he paid too much since he bought the property. "My taxes went up over $2,000 in one year, but the assessor's taxes had not gone up in 12 years."

Jeff told his cousin who also lived in the town about the dubious assessment practices. Together, they contacted their state representative. The representative came to town and Jeff and his cousin showed him some of the questionable property record cards. The representative admitted that there was "something wrong here," and asked Jeff and his cousin to get 15-20 names on a petition which requested an investigation of the questionable assessing practices in the town. Jeff got his representative 90 names and for some reason, "the representative blew his stack and said angrily that he didn't want 90 names." Jeff gave a copy of the petition to his selectman and Jeff told him that "they want to bury this." Jeff got in touch with me and that is when I wrote the infamous letter to the DOR that included the 90 named petition asking for the DOR to investigate the "irregularities" in the assessor's office. A copy of the letter is provided at the end of the chapter.

The Department of Revenue did come to the town and discovered irregularities in the town's assessments. However, it was not enough for Jeff that the DOR investigated the assessor's office. "They had been signing off on these wrong numbers for years. I called the head of local services and told her that I will come to Boston and park my ass on her doorstep with a big sign until she does something about these assessors. I told her she will have to come up with an explanation for the press. I had nothing to lose and everything to gain." The official told Jeff that an outside agency would do the re-assessments in his town. She asked Jeff, "What do you want me to do?" He responded, "The assessors committed tax fraud. I want you to put them in jail." The official told Jeff to calm down and that this would all get worked out. Jeff summed it up, "But it's not worked out. This is going on all over the state."

These horror stories are occurring all over the country. In Arizona, a real estate agent recounted a problem a client of hers had with the property tax system in her state. Elaborating, "This man was from Greece and had purchased property here in the Phoenix area. When I saw his tax bill, I was surprised how high it was and suggested that he appeal it. Now this was a very savvy, international businessman. He told me that he started the appeals process, but found it so complicated that he could not figure out what to do and he ended up going back to Greece."

People of good conscience also tried to right the wrongs perpetrated by many assessors. Good neighbors who spoke out on behalf of others getting screwed by their assessors often felt the backlash on their next valuation. When a long time resident saw a newcomer receive an unfair assessment and spoke out at a town meeting, the assessors were at her house the very next day with a tape measure in hand. The assessors proceeded to visit her home 6 times and raised her valuation 55% in one year. Although she won her case at the ATB, she knew that the assessors would punish her and jack up her assessment the following year. This is exactly what happened. Tired of having to fight the assessors EVERY YEAR, this woman put her house on the market and hopes to find a better community with honest assessors.

Another good-hearted Samaritan who questioned the assessors' ethics found his farm had been removed from an agricultural designation and his taxes tripled. Unable to pay his new tax bill, he was not allowed by law to file for an abatement and fight the removal from an agricultural designation. The assessors also spread slanderous stories about the farmer and damaged his reputation which turned other residents against him. This is another example of an unregulated system that allows assessors to exact financial and emotional revenge at their whim.

Semi-retired newcomers to a Midwest town were faced with wildly out of control assessors who entered fraudulent data on their property record card which increased the couple's annual property tax bill by over $35,000! Although this assessment was outrageous and erroneous, the property owners had to pay the entire tax bill or lose their right to appeal. According to the Johnsons' attorney, these assessors knowingly falsified the property record card entries, which doubled the actual size of the home. Unbelievably, when confronted with proof of the fraudulent entries, the assessors refused to correct them! "This was a case of assessors gone mad," explained their attorney.

The Johnson's won their case and exposed high level corruption with this Board of Assessors. As it turned out, these assessors gave themselves, their friends and family, extremely low assessments and then targeted approximately 15% of the population for over-valuation to make up the difference. When this was revealed to the public, the Johnson's lives were threatened. Apparently there were some who did not want to lose their "privilege" of lowball assessments or for some whose property was mysteriously not even on the tax rolls, the "privilege" of no assessment at all.

You might query, "Why not use the democratic process and vote the assessors out?" With the elected assessors giving 85% of the voters a low assessment, there was no hope of ever voting them out of office. Just another curious fact from property tax hell. The Johnson's have the distinction of successfully winning their appeal, but they continue to be shadowed by angry assessors who are out for revenge.

The elderly, many on fixed incomes with limited resources, find themselves at particular risk when it comes to property taxes. Anne contacted us about her elderly neighbors who own a home that is a mirror image to hers. "They live one street over from me and their home is in a state of disrepair. I keep my home up and just renovated my kitchen, but their home is valued at $100,000 more than mine! I believe that the assessors did that because they know the elderly couple will not question their assessment," she explained sadly.

Probably the most heinous case that was brought to our attention is the case involving a 91 year-old taxpayer from a small town whom we shall call, "Nancy." This taxpayer was awaiting the completion of the sale of 25 acres of her land to the state of Massachusetts. This land had been designated forestry land and by law, received a tax benefit. In 2003, while the sale was pending, this resident, 87 at the time, sustained a broken hip that required hospitalization. Still hospitalized, Nancy did not receive full payment from the state for her land. Instead, she received a partial payment from the state and was sent a copy of a check that was sent to the town's assessors for $14,317.97. She was still too ill to act upon the fact that she had been shorted money on the sale of her land.

When Nancy recovered, she confronted the town's assessors and asked about the $14,317.97 paid to the town. The assessors told Nancy that the town took the money for roll-back taxes. The truth is, however, that with land sold to the state and kept in the same forestry designation, roll-back taxes were not owed. Upset, Nancy contacted the state's attorney and inquired why the state sent a check for $14,317.97 to the town. This attorney verified that no roll-back taxes were owed and told this elderly taxpayer to ask the assessors. It is a disgrace that this attorney did not intervene to help this elderly woman.

Nancy, as is common with a good deal of our elderly citizens, always paid her taxes on time and in full every year. Nothing was owed to this town. Obviously upset, Nancy sought redress and asked the assessors for an abatement form to contest the imposition of these illegal taxes. The assessors refused to give this elderly woman the abatement form. Nancy wrote and called the assessors; a courtesy of a response was never given. She continued her letter writing campaign until her death in 2007. She was 91.

The executrix of Nancy's estate picked up the flag and continued to fight for the return of the $14,317.97. During her investigation, she uncovered two illegal "withdrawal tax liens" crafted by the assessors and notorized by the town clerk. In June of 2008, the executrix called the state's attorney and wanted an explanation regarding the $14,317.97. She was told that in order for the sale to go through, the state had to make out a check to the town for alleged back taxes. Aghast, the executrix told the attorney that the taxes were always paid in a timely manner and no back taxes were owed. It is obvious where this misinformation came from. The executrix asked why Nancy was never advised of the fact that the town was alleging that back taxes were owed and she received this answer, "Oh, she was too ill." The fact of the matter is that nobody expected Nancy to survive and her death would have hidden the illegality of the town's activities. But she did survive and complained to her assessors as she was instructed by the state's attorney; all to no avail. The $14,317.97 was never recovered from the town. This abuse of power regarding this elderly taxpayer is just simply despicable.

Assessor abuse cuts across all class lines and the wealthy are not immune from assessor corruption. Elton John's Atlanta condominium was overassessed by almost one million dollars. Apparently he was not the only one targeted. The county residents consistently complained to their assessors and representatives that the tax valuations of their homes bore little resemblance to their actual market values. After an audit that was critical of the assessors, three of the five assessors resigned. All across the country, there are similar stories of overassessment and wealth does not protect a taxpayer from assessor abuse and negligence. Perhaps the system is too broken to fix.

Problems with untrained and sometimes unscrupulous assessors are not confined to property owners. Trouble has also been reported by certified appraisers. The certified appraisers that spoke with us are some of the most highly trained in the country and truly know the business of assessing. One appraiser from the mid-west who trains assessors reported this event with a newly elected assessor. "This older woman came to my class with her girlfriend. She hadn't the slightest interest in becoming an assessor, but some people in town got together and wrote her name on the ballot and she won the election. This newly elected assessor and her girlfriend talked through the entire class. I asked her somewhat sarcastically, 'Would you like for me to set up a table in the back of the room so that you and your friend can continue to talk uninterrupted?' Unbelievably she replied, 'Yes, we would really like that!' So I set up a table for both of them and they continued to talk through the entire week of class! When I gave the class a test, there was a math question regarding assessment and her answer was, 'This makes my brain hurt.' Another question on comparable assessments asked if this was the correct valuation amount. Her answer was, 'I don't know, but I think it's too high.' Unfortunately, where assessors are elected this may be the person who is assessing your property and holds your home's financial future in his or her hands."

Other certified appraisers told us of assessors who had vendettas against property owners and affixed their valuations obscenely high. One certified appraiser stated, "In one case, I confronted the assessor and he absolutely refused to adjust the valuation to its proper amount. Due to the property tax laws in Illinois, there was nothing I could do to change the value. I filed the abatement for the property owner, called him to tell him what had happened and instructed him to follow the appeals process as he had been singled out for unfair taxation. Unfortunately, when an assessor is elected, they wield too much power, in my opinion, and property owners can find themselves on the short end of a very long stick, facing a long drawn out appeals process, filing and attorney fees."

"Another certified licensed appraiser stated 'the computer did it,' is my biggest pet peeve with assessors who take my training classes. I tell them, if 'the computer did it,' it must be so much smarter than you, then you better bring that computer up here to the front of the class so we can all take a look at it." As this appraiser explained further, "There is no such thing as 'the computer did it.' Every number must be justified by the assessors. If they don't have the answers, then they had better find them. Taxpayers deserve total transparency. They need to know how every number on their record card is derived and how it impacts their property tax bill," he added adamantly.

Sometimes, it is just the property tax system itself that is at fault. In Texas, a woman contacted us about the home that she and her husband purchased for $750,000. "We worked hard, scrimped and saved to purchase our 'dream home.' We have no credit card debt and live frugally," she explained. Their property tax bill, which was once affordable, had now tripled in two years and this woman tearfully told us, "Our property taxes are so high and out of control that I can no longer afford to live here. We are being forced to sell our home in a down market and will most likely lose everything we worked so hard to achieve." There is something terribly wrong with a system of taxation that drives financially responsible people from their homes.

While this couple in Texas struggled to pay their exorbitant property taxes that will leave them homeless, a Detroit Councilwoman paid almost no taxes, ($68 per year), on her upscale home for ten years or more. Meanwhile, her neighbors' homes had property tax bills ranging between $2,100 and $6,400 annually. The Councilwoman pleaded ignorance on the issue and when the news hit the press, she offered to pay back some of the taxes. This is just another reason to get rid of a property tax system that doesn't know the meaning of the phrase, "equal taxation under the law."

In New York, 51 taxpayers banded together to fight assessor abuse in their town. They filed suit against the town complaining that they were unfairly targeted because they were newcomers. One homeowner's taxes increased by $3,000 in one year. Another taxpayer's home was scheduled for demolition because it was unlivable; it was assessed for $317,381. These taxpayers, represented by counsel, argued that their taxes are unconstitutional, unlawful and arbitrary. In the words of the attorney, "the system is flawed." It appears that the word is getting out. It's time for a change.

These horror stories are commonplace and indicative of a system that has failed us all. More often than not, people have been told that the system is fair and equitable. Yet, nothing could be further from the truth. There are no enforced checks and balances and this leads to disparate assessments and unconstitutionally applied property taxes. As one irate property taxpayer stated, "Let's stop pretending that this system is fair. Why not just tell it like it is? The system is rigged against us and the assessors can value property at their whim." We deserve the truth.

PATRICIA QUINTILIAN
Attorney at Law

October 4, 2006

Massachusetts Department of Revenue
██████████████, Chief
P.O. Box 9569
Boston, MA 02114-9569

Re: Town of ██████ Certification

Dear Ms. ██████:

I am formally requesting that the Department of Revenue
investigate the Town of ██████'s assessment procedures. I, as
well as many taxpayers and voters, have serious concerns about
the town assessors' capabilities to assess the properties in the
Town of ██████.[1] See Exhibit I attached hereto. Past
irregularities in town assessment procedures and concomitant
assessments require an investigation to ascertain whether the
Town of ██████ was improperly certified.

I have previously verbalized my concerns to Mr. ████████████
of the Office of the Taxpayer Advocate. Additionally, I and
several taxpayers have communicated our concerns to the Town of
████████ selectman (Selectmen ████████, ████████ and
████████) via a public town meeting. Moreover, these concerns
were also communicated to Representative ████████ and it is
my understanding that he has verbalized the ████████ residents'
concerns directly to you and requested that the Department of
Revenue look into the matter. If this is not the case, I would
appreciate a response to clarify the matter for me.

As you well know, the commissioner shall enforce all laws
relating to the valuation, classification and assessment of
property and shall supervise the administration of such laws by
local assessors in accordance with the rules, regulations and
guidelines established under the law. G.L.c.58 § 1A.

---

[1] The enclosed signatory sheets are just a small sampling of the taxpayers in
██████. Of all the people canvassed, only two refused to sign because of
concerns of reprisal.

41

Massachusetts Department of Revenue
█████████, Chief
October 4, 2006
Page Two

The assessors of each city and town shall determine the fair
cash valuation of such real property for the purpose of
taxation. G.L.c.59 § 2A. The law requires that fair cash value
is determined by "arm's length" market sales and is effectuated
by equalized assessed valuation ratios (EQV ratio).

The law requires that real property must be assessed equitably.
I am placing the Department of Revenue on notice that some of
the assessments for the Town of █████ are not assessed at their
fair cash value and that the EQV ratios have not been uniformly
implemented within the classifications of residential homes.

As you well know, the Department of Revenue simply does not have
the resources or man power to adequately supervise the
assessments on an individual basis. The DOR simply does random
checking within the classifications. G.L.c.58 § 10. As such,
this is formal notification that the assessment for the Town of
█████ simply does not fall within the confines of well
established law regarding assessments.

More specifically, with respect to my residence located at █████
█████████, █████, for the tax year of 2002, I objected to the
assessment performed by the assessors and their failure to
properly determine the square footage of my residence.[2] The
appellate tax board ruled the fair cash value of my home as
$241,600 for tax year 2002. The █████ assessors for the
following year of 2003, raised the total valuation of my home by
$114,000, to $355,600, an increase of 47% in one year. See
Exhibit II. Not only is there no increase even close for this
year within the classification of contemporary homes as per the
assessor's classification, there is no increase even close for
any property in any classification in the entire town for the
year of 2003. See Exhibit III.

Moreover, for this very same year, inexplicably, the town
assessor's argued and introduced to the appellate tax board that
they valued my residence at $274,700 for fiscal year 2003. See
Exhibit II marked as exhibit 2 by the board. Eight months later,
the same assessors assessed and billed me for my home assessed

---

[2] The error in square footage will be addressed further in the letter with
supportive documentation.

Massachusetts Department of Revenue
█████████, Chief
October 4, 2006
Page Three

at **$355,600** for the same fiscal year of 2003. See Exhibit II. No improvements were performed and there is simply no rational explanation for two field cards with such a disparity in assessment for the same year.

On its face, these actions do not comport with EQV ratios. Nor is there any rational reason or justification for raising my assessment **47%** in one year when there were no improvements of any kind made on the residence. The only reasonable explanation is that the increase was retributive and done to deter me from exercising my rights under the law by appealing to the appellate tax board. If this reason is excluded, the only logical remaining conclusion is that the assessors are simply not qualified to carry out the duties of assessing for the Town of ██████.

More notable however is that for the tax year 2002, I was the fifth highest assessed property for the **entire town and for all classifications.** At the time this case was pending before the Appellate Tax Board, I attempted to get this information prior to the hearing. I was told by Assessor ████████ that this information was too burdensome to obtain and this was verified in the Town's answers to interrogatories. In 2006, I obtained the enclosed blue booklet information from a taxpayer who obtained it in 2002 and 2003 from the same assessor, Ms. ██████.

Most disturbing however is the comparative homes that I was grouped in, **5 and 6 bedroom** homes. See Exhibit IV. For the following year, 2003, my assessment was the **third highest** for all classifications in the entire town. Exhibit IV. Again, there is simply no rational reason for my assessment increase when there was absolutely no improvements made on my home. Again, the assessment on my home for tax year 2003 was retributive.

In 2006, I attempted to get the information for tax years 2004 and 2005 and was denied the information by the assessors and was told that they could not access the computer for those years. As incredulous as this may seem, it is verified by further information that taxpayers are being told that "if they file for an abatement, then somebody else would have to pay their share of taxes." Another taxpayer was told that he had too much money

Massachusetts Department of Revenue
████████████, Chief
October 4, 2006
Page Four

and could not file for his senior discount for being over 70. These taxpayers are afraid of retribution by the assessors and would not allow me to disclose their names, but they would talk to a representative from the Department of Revenue if their identities would not be disclosed to the assessors. This kind of behavior should not be countenanced by inaction on the part of the DOR.

Moreover, I have attempted to obtain information by the appraisal company retained by the Town of ████████ to ascertain the company's assessment practices and advice given to the Town assessors. I have been denied this information by the Town of ████████ as well as the appraisal company retained by the town. The appraisal company has refused to comply with my subpoena to disclose the information to me. This company has been listed by the DOR on its website with a disclaimer: ████████████ & Associates, ████████████████████████████. I find this entire refusal to disclose public records very disturbing.

Additionally, the EQV ratios have not been uniformly implemented within the classifications of the residential homes. I have enclosed the classification of contemporary homes from 2003-2006. See Exhibit V. As you can see, there are very disturbing examples of individual homes within the classification that are way out of line. The obvious exclusions because of improvements were not part of the evaluation as properly noted. These discrepancies, my home and several others are not within the classification's standard increase as determined by the EQV ratios. The land increase percentage is also perplexing for several properties. Moreover, I questioned assistant assessor Mr. ████████ regarding the standard assessment for a building lot for the Town of ████████ and was told that there wasn't a standard assessment for a building lot and that he would have to look it up in the computer. I am perplexed over the misinformation that I have been getting from the assessor's office.

The aforementioned information is just the tip of the iceberg with regard to the certification of the Town of ████████ by the DOR. Within the classification as determined by the Town of ████████[3], (contemporary) the certification sheet as utilized and

---

[3] The Town of ████████ assessor's determined that a geodesic dome is classified as contemporary.

Massachusetts Department of Revenue
███████, Chief
October 4, 2006
Page Five

reviewed by the DOR has an almost identical residence building
to my residence, ██████████████. See Exhibit VI. My home is
determined as average and the identical comparative (███████
████████) is valued as good, and yet my building is almost
$20,000 dollars above the building assessment of the comparative
████████████ Road building.

Furthermore, there are many, many, other examples of strange
assessments in the other classifications. More specifically, a
taxpayer who owns property at ██████████████ in █████ has a
home **without electricity or running water and has an out house.**
This property cannot be accessed via the town road, yet this
property is assessed at $150,300. See Exhibit VII. The building
is valued at $51,700. One of the assessor's home, ████████
(building) has all of the modern amenities and is assessed at
$90,700 and is located on the main road in █████. See Exhibit
VIII.

Furthermore, with regards to this property, the taxpayer was
assessed $9,000 for a **41** year old pole barn with a dirt floor
that is completely out of square and plum.[4] Upset, this taxpayer
questioned his assessment for the barn. This taxpayer was aware
of the fact that Assessor █████ assessed her own detached
building at $4,500. Her building is a Morton building with a
foundation, electricity and a full cement floor. When questioned
about this obvious unfairness, Ms. ██████ responded, "a wooden
building was more valuable than a metal building." After this
discussion in the spring of 2006 during the certification
process, Assessor ████████ assessment for her Morton building
mysteriously increased to $10,000. See Exhibit VIII. This
taxpayer is extremely upset with the assessment of his and many
other properties in the town and would like to speak with a DOR
representative.

In 2006, another taxpayer was assessed $23,500 for his pole barn
that was built in 1974 and is 28 by 50 feet with a slab floor.
Exhibit IX. The town assessor's sons, █████ and ██████████,
were assessed for a pole barn that was built in 1989 and is 42
by 60 feet and it is assessed at $16,300. Exhibit IX. There is
running water, a bathroom, shower, and office in the assessor's

---

[4] This can be confirmed by the assistant assessor, Mr. ████, who has since
resigned from his position.

Massachusetts Department of Revenue
███████████, Chief
October 4, 2006
Page Six

sons' pole barn. The obvious unfairness in this assessment is
self evident in this case. This taxpayer is very upset with this
obvious disparity in treatment. There are many more examples of
unequal assessment in the Town of ████████. This taxpayer would
also like the opportunity to speak with a DOR representative.

Furthermore, the assessor's own properties are highly suspect
with regard to their evaluations for the past several years. See
Exhibit VIII. Assessor ██████████ bought his property in 1992 for
$66,500. For the next **10 years**, his total assessment for
building and land increased a mere **$2,000**. A review of his
assessment history and failure to raise his assessments as the
other good taxpayers of the Town of ████████ taxes were raised in
the height of the real estate boom is perplexing and warrants
further investigation.

Furthermore, there is more than enough evidence to question the
professional capabilities of the assessors to properly carry out
their public duties. More specifically, I have built a geodesic
dome which is a ten sided figure. I have been telling the
assessor's that they have not properly figured the square
footage of the domes. As an ex-science teacher with degrees in
biology and psychology, it is self evident that they erred in
their evaluation of the square footage. See Exhibit II. Please
note that they have the dome garage first floor at 924 square
feet and the second floor at 924 square feet. It is common sense
that this is not a dome.

In an effort to get the assessors to listen to reason, I
retained a structural engineer who builds domes to tell them
that their square footage is off. See Exhibit X. To my and the
engineer's absolute dismay, the assessor's have refused to
rectify this very obvious error. The assessors' ineptitude has
cost me $750. More importantly, the engineer confirmed the
square footage using a CAD program for geodesic domes and by
using the proper mathematical formulas. I have repeatedly asked
the Appellate Tax Board to help in this matter and the judge
has, every year, told me that he cannot address this issue. It
is a DOR issue. Obviously, square footage impacts assessment and
value. I am asking that this very obvious error be rectified
immediately.

██████████, Chief
October 4, 2006
Page Seven

Furthermore, I have reviewed the assessments of other geodesic
domes in Western Massachusetts and have ascertained that the
Town of ██████ is way off in its assessment of my dome. A date
sheet of newly built geodesic domes and older domes in the area
is enclosed for your review. Exhibit XI. Of particular note is
the almost identical dome in ████████. The only difference is
that the dome is five years newer than mine and in better
condition, but has less square footage. It appears that the
surrounding assessors are getting it right, the notable
exception is the Town of ██████.

It is self evident that this information warrants an
investigation by the DOR to ascertain whether the certification
of the Town of ██████ should be revoked. Furthermore, under the
law, the commissioner can cause an assessor to be prosecuted for
any violation of law relative to assessment or classification of
taxes for which a penalty is imposed. G.L.C. 58 § 1A. I am
requesting that this information be forwarded to your
investigatory unit of the DOR for investigation of potential
violations of the law. If you do not have an enforcement
department, please advise and I will forward this information to
the Office of the Attorney General for potential violations of
the law.

I thank you for your anticipated efforts in evaluating the
enclosed information and am requesting that a written response
as to whether the DOR will take any action with regard to our
requests. In light of the ongoing problems that have plagued the
Town's assessment procedures for many years, a prompt reply
would be appreciated by all of the disgruntled taxpayers in the
Town of ██████.

Sincerely,

Patricia Quintilian
Attorney at Law

PAQ/al
Enclosures
Cc: Commissioner ████████
     Deputy Commissioner ████████
     Representative ████████

Chapter Five
How To Read Your Property Record Card, Cost Value Report Or Pricing Ladder

I hold in my hand 1,379 pages of tax simplification
~ Delbert L. Latta

Your property record card is your key to understanding your home's assessed value. Property record cards are generated by a variety of software programs. Each city or town has its own software assessment program that generates your property record card information. Software programs vary from town to town and state to state, and each program generates a different format. You must find out what program your city or town utilizes so that you can decode your property record card. Massachusetts, for example, uses five software programs: CAMA (Computer Assisted Mass Appraisal); Patriot Properties; Vision Appraisal Technology; Kapinos Associates; and CLT Appraisal & Assessment Services. The abbreviations on your property record cards will depend upon which computer program your town uses. You can find the program that your town uses by looking on your property record card. If for some strange reason it is not listed on your property record card, then contact your assessor's office and ask what program they use. The abbreviations for the various programs are provided at the end of this chapter.

The format of your property record card will be uniform for all properties in your town or city. The classification of the property type will be uniform for all of the computer programs in your state. Several examples of property type classifications are "residential", "commercial", "agricultural", "multiple use", "chapter 61 lands", etc. The property type classification "use codes" can be found on the Department of Revenue's web site. For Massachusetts, the link can be found here:

http://www.mass.gov/Ador/docs/dls/bla/classificationcodebook.pdf
For your state's codes please go to "FIND YOUR STATE:"
http://www.propertytaxrights.com/index.php?option=com_wrapper &view=wrapper&Itemid=119
The state "use codes" are also listed at the end of this chapter.

Regardless of what computer program your town uses in generating your property record card, your first step is to review your card for any and all errors. For example, check the number of bedrooms, bathrooms, garage capacity, fireplaces, etc. You should check the square footage of each floor, basement, deck, etc. of your home. A few anecdotal stories of glaring assessor mistakes are provided for illustrative purposes:

1. A homeowner was assessed for a sixteen-car garage; the homeowner had a two-car garage.

2. A homeowner had one fireplace, but was assessed for three.

3. 1,000 square feet was incorrectly added to an A-frame home's top level.

4. A homeowner was assessed for a non-existent building.

These obvious errors should have been noticed by the assessor. All of these errors incorrectly increased these homes' assessed values and these taxpayers paid taxes they did not owe.

If you are not in the habit of reviewing your property record card, you may suffer the consequences and pay more than your fair share of property taxes every year. The moral of the story is clear – you are 100% responsible for checking the accuracy of all entries made by the assessors on your property record card. If there is something you do not understand or the entry seems arbitrary, ask your assessors to explain the entries to you. After all, according to the DOR, "accurate property data is essential for developing uniform valuations of comparable properties in a mass appraisal program."

The next step is to determine what assessment method your assessors used to determine the assessed value of your home. In Massachusetts, the assessors are required to assess your home at its "fair cash value" as of the first day of January of each year.[4] Generally, assessors, real estate valuation experts and the courts rely upon three approaches to determine the fair cash value of your home: income capitalization, sales comparison, and cost reproduction.[5]

The sales comparison and cost approach are the most common methods used by assessors. The sales comparison or market approach is the most commonly used, and as such, will be covered in depth in this book. The cost reproduction approach is simply the current cost to replace the building minus depreciation due to age or condition. The land value is separately determined by using the sales comparison approach. Usually, each city or town has a standard assessed value for a building lot and then adjusts the value of additional land by a standard value for each additional acre above the building lot acreage. The

[4] M.G.L. c. 59, § 38.
[5] Correia v. New Bedford Redevelopment Authority, 375 Mass. 360, 362 (1978).

income approach to valuation or capitalization approach is used predominantly in the valuation of commercial/industrial properties and rental properties. The assessors estimate the rental income from a property and capitalize that income into an estimate of current value.

The cost approach to valuation is based upon published cost manuals that develop building costs and depreciation tables. The widely used firm of Marshall & Swift, who identify themselves as "the building cost people," publish a manual titled *Marshall & Swift Cost Analysis*. These manuals are routinely used by real estate professionals such as appraisers, assessors, lenders and tax consultants when using the cost reproduction approach. Marshall & Swift's tables value everything from construction costs per square foot, to siding, roofing, heating and cooling systems, etc. Costs are catalogued and listed by zip code. More than likely, if your town uses a cost approach to valuing your home, your town's assessing software is based on Marshall & Swift's tables. More information can be found at www.marshallswift.com. Marshall & Swift's tables are invaluable and you can compare your assessor's cost analysis to theirs. Bear in mind that each town or citywide software system that your assessor uses, (i.e. CAMA), may allow input for their own idiosyncrasies specific to your area. However, for general comparisons, Marshall & Swift is a solid point of reference.

If your town uses the cost approach for assessment, ask for the Cost Value Report or Pricing Ladder, which is a detailed breakdown of the value of every item or characteristic of your house such as heating systems, air conditioning, roofing, number of bathrooms, bathroom fixtures, number of fireplaces, etc. This document and your property record card should give you the information necessary to figure out how the assessors arrived at the assessed value of your property. When using the cost approach, depreciation must be subtracted from the Replacement Cost New (RCN) or the building cost. The resultant number is abbreviated as "RCNLD" or Replacement Cost New Less Depreciation. This number is the assessed value of your building.

The most commonly used appraisal approach is the market approach to assessment. For information on how assessors in Massachusetts use this approach to adjust assessed values to reflect market values, see the following manual at this link:

http://www.mass.gov/Ador/docs/dls/publ/101Handbook/coverand toc.pdf

This manual, "Assessment Administration: Law Procedures and Valuation Course," will give you an idea of the assessors' practices with regard to assessing your home.

The market approach uses the sales prices of comparable properties that are sold in close proximity to the assessment date. Once "arm's-length" sales have been identified, assessors must conduct a sales analysis of the current market and assessed property values within the town and identify any valuation adjustments that need to be made. Houses sold through "arm's-length" transactions or sales are when the buyer and seller have no relationship and the sale is under no duress. Homes that are sold as part of a foreclosure, a "short sale," a divorce settlement, or part of an inheritance are not "arm's-length" transactions. The accuracy of this approach is dependent upon the statistical adequacy of comparable sales. The market analysis may be performed by the assessors or their consultant and the resultant data and market adjustments are entered into the town's computer program. These computer programs have the ability to apply market changes to all comparable properties within the city or town.

After you have checked your property record card for mistakes, there are several areas where assessors have total discretion to make their own subjective judgments regarding your property, which can significantly increase your assessment. Regardless of what program your town uses, each program leaves enormous discretion to the assessors and with a few keystrokes, your value can go from reasonable and accurate to irrational and flawed. For example, each program uses the term "condition" to evaluate your building or its sub-parts such as the condition of your bathroom, kitchen, fireplace, etc. Obviously, "condition" is a judgment call that can affect your entire assessed value. Inferior quality or condition lowers your valuation. There are no hard and fast rules for this category and one assessor's "good" may be another assessor's "average."

An attorney recently told me of a conversation he had with a local assessor. He asked the assessor, "How do you decide if a property is fair, good, or below average?" The assessor responded with, "I have my own system." The attorney asked, "What is it based on?" The assessor replied, "Have you ever seen the movie, 'TEN'?" Incredulous, the attorney asked for more details. The assessor explained that his system was simply based on the movie and that he also decided property conditions and other characteristics based upon how he was feeling that day. This is a prime example of a property tax system that grants enormous latitude to assessors. This systemic discretionary power is a breeding ground for unequal taxation. Another subjective call that can make for a very big increase or decrease at the assessor's discretion is the "Grade" of your home. "Grade" is the type of construction used for your home—i.e. is this a pre-fab home or designed by architects with fine materials? This is the assessors' call.

Not only do assessors have discretion to evaluate the "Condition" and "Grade" of your home, but they can also adjust items that are seemingly immune to discretionary power. For example, a resident discovered that her heating system "cost" on her "Cost Value Report" was twice what Marshall & Swift recommended for her zip code and house style, and twice what she actually paid for it. When this homeowner further examined her assessor's radiant floor heating "cost" however, she found it had an amount vastly under the Marshall & Swift building "cost." Our researchers were able to uncover multiple discrepancies comparing Marshall & Swift tables to Assessor generated Cost Value Reports. In many cases the construction costs per square foot were so random that it implied the tables were not used at all. In one zip code, construction costs varied between $42 per square foot to $250 per square foot all within similar home styles and similar construction materials. There was absolutely no rhyme or reason to any of the costs attributed to these homes. So check and re-check every single figure and compare your figures to Marshall & Swift or another construction cost table. Also, compare your assessors' cost value reports on their own properties to yours. Lastly, compare your cost value reports to other similarly situated homes.

If you were involved in the construction of your home and have your actual building cost receipts, you can compare the receipts to the information on your property record card and Cost Value Report or Pricing Ladder. You must go through your property record card with a fine tooth comb and look at every cost they are attributing to your home.

On two towns' record cards, our researchers found a mysterious "Market Adjustment" entry. Actually, what made this mysterious is that there was no entry in this category – it was blank. Our math wizards figured out that these assessors were using a 1.2497 market adjustment number to increase the property owners' valuation. This market adjustment was on every property record card in the town. But why?

Our researchers questioned the Department of Revenue on this market adjustment number and received the following reply:

> *"The multiplier is determined by the municipality. However, the majority of municipalities use one of the commonly accepted manuals, such as The Marshall Swift Cost Manual (http://www.marshallswift.com/). For more information regarding the rest of your questions as to how the multiplier is determined, I suggest you get a copy of one of these manuals."*

Our researchers then spoke to Marshall & Swift and were told that a market adjustment number applied to an entire town is used for special circumstances such as when the location is an island or a resort. In these kinds of cases, the construction costs of the homes are increased because it is more expensive to get building supplies to the location. The research team also spoke with assessors in surrounding towns in the same state and were told that they had not used a market adjustment number in many years. Another assessor in a town that was still using the market adjustment number said that they had used the number to adjust assessments because the market sales had been so much higher than the valuations. However, they were told by the DOR to stop using the market adjustment number. Another town that was still using the market adjustment number gave us the unacceptable answer that "the computer did it."

How do you know if your town is using this market adjustment factor? You cannot rely on simply reading your property record card to find out because shockingly, it may not be noted on the card. For example, there was an RCNLD number entered for a property owner's home at $148,115, the building cost number was $185,100 and that was the number the assessors used as the taxable total. There was no entry in "market adjustment" and no explanation from the assessors. In this example, this town did in fact use a market adjustment factor and failed to reveal it on the property record card. The lesson here is that you must ask in every single case if your assessors are factoring in a "market adjustment" to arrive at your taxable total.

Also, check the year entered on your property record card that your house was built. Note that there is a "Year Built" category and an "Effective Year Built" category. The "Year Built" is the year that construction began. The "Effective Year Built" is the year that construction was completed or the home had improvements or was renovated. Your home should be depreciated from the "Effective Year Built."

We checked record cards in a town and found only two record cards that had an "Effective Year Built" entry. There were many property owners who had renovated their homes. None of these homeowners had any notation on their property record cards documenting these renovations. For example, one home built in 1945 and completely renovated in 1998 received depreciation based on the year 1945. There was only an entry for "Year Built" (1945), and no entry for "Effective Year Built," (which should have said 1998). If depreciation was being applied fairly, either all property owners would have depreciation applied on "Year Built" or all who had undergone renovations and multi-year construction would have "Depreciation" on "Effective Year Built."Depreciation rates are much greater for homes built in 1945, so this property owner received a huge decrease in his assessed value. The two property owners with "Effective Year Built" entries did not get the depreciation that the rest of the town was getting and were therefore "getting screwed."

The import of checking your property record card cannot be overstated. An assessor who took over the assessing duties in a town recently advised me that she uncovered over a million dollars in assessing errors since she took office. Unfortunately, these kinds of errors appear to be the norm rather than the exception. During our research of one town's property record cards, it appeared that the assessors were giving value to each property FIRST and then manipulating the data to support the value the assessors wanted it to have! Everything from square footage to rooms to condition were adjusted to fit the value chosen by the assessors, rather than assessing the property based on how many rooms, how much square footage, etc. was ACTUALLY THERE! Frightening, but true. Of course, the proper way to assess is to enter accurate data into the system and then let the software produce a taxable total.

How does one check on the assessor's methodology and accuracy? By law, the assessors must ensure that all properties within a town or city are valued uniformly and equitably. In order to ensure uniformity and fairness, assessors can use appraisal methodology that incorporates standard statistical analysis. There are several questions and assessments that you can use to ascertain whether you are being treated fairly. The most useful measure of appraisal uniformity is the term "Coefficient of Dispersion." In other words, the Coefficient of Dispersion tells you how far your home's value is from the median. This term basically measures the deviation of sales from the "Assessment to Sales Ratio" or "ASR" within a specified class or subclass such as style of homes, age, location, condition, etc. The ASR is a mathematical calculation found by dividing the assessed value by the sales price. Let's say your home was purchased for $200,000 and it is assessed at $200,000. Your ASR will be 1.00. An ASR of 1.00 represents market value. An ASR below 1.00 indicates the property is assessed for less than its market value. An ASR above 1.00 indicates the property is assessed for more than its market value. All residential subclasses, (contemporary, ranch, colonial, etc.) must have ASRs between 90-110% and the ASRs must be within 5% of each other. Massachusetts guidelines require the Coefficient of Dispersion to be 10% or under for single family residential homes. An acceptable range for the Coefficient of Dispersion is between 5 and 8. If the COD is high, the assessments are not uniform and there is an error somewhere. You can check on any class or subclass by consulting Chapter Two of the Assessment Administration: Law Procedures and Valuation Course which can be found on line at the DOR web site. All of the formulas and examples can be found in this manual:

http://www.mass.gov/Ador/docs/dls/publ/101Handbook/coverand toc.pdf

Another report that you can request from you assessor is called the "current to previous ratio report." It is a comparison of the current and previous year assessments for a particular class or subclass, for example, the style of your home. The ratio exemplifies the change in assessments between the years. If there is no change, you will see a number "1." If the assessment increased, you will see an increase above "1;" a decrease in assessment will warrant a number under "1." You can then compare the increase or decrease for all of the homes within your style of homes.

Moreover, in order to have equality and fairness in property taxation, the homes within a certain style of homes such as contemporary, colonial, ranch, etc., should have the same percentage increase in assessment from year to year if there were no changes made to the property such as a new addition, porch, etc. For example, if you have a ranch style home, with no recent additions or renovations and your value has risen 10%, then check to see if all of the other ranches in your neighborhood/town have also risen 10%. Please note that you are evaluating the percentage of increase or decrease in assessment, not the total assessment from property to property. For example, your ranch style home was valued at $200,000 last year and is valued at $240,000 this year – an increase of 20%. When you look at your neighbor, John Doe's ranch style home, you discover that it was valued at $250,000 last year, and is $262,500 this year, which illustrates a 5% increase. This can be the beginning of a very strong case for lowering your assessment. You should now request a report from the assessors of all ranch style homes in your town and compare their percentage increase in valuation to yours. If you live in a large city, this list can be overwhelmingly lengthy. If that is your situation, then limit your request to your style of home within a few neighborhoods, age of the home, or similar characteristics. The percentage increase within your style of home category should be the same for each building within this sample if there were no changes done to the home. If the assessors were assessing your class or subclass properly, the percentage of increase or decrease should be uniform for all the buildings throughout the class.

Following the steps described above and summarized at the end of this chapter, you should be able to tell whether your assessment is accurate and based upon sound appraisal methodology. If not, you should file for an abatement (a decrease in the assessed value of your property). The procedure to file for an abatement is covered in Chapter Six, "The Legal Process—Where Do You Begin?"

STEPS:

1. Find out what software system your assessors used.
2. Find out what appraisal methodology they used in assessing your home.
3. If you do not understand the codes on your property record card and Cost Value Report or Pricing Ladder, ask your assessors for clarification or contact a Certified Appraiser.
4. Check your record card and Cost Value Report or Pricing Ladder for ACCURACY.
5. Check your record card and Cost Value Report or Pricing Ladder against other record cards of similar homes in your neighborhood and town.
6. If the assessors live in your town, check their record cards and Cost Value Report or Pricing Ladder.
7. If you were involved in the construction of your home and have an accounting of costs, compare them to the cost analysis provided by your assessors. You can also do a cost analysis of your home with Marshall & Swift's online estimator and compare that to the cost analysis provided by your assessors.
8. Make detailed notes of all discrepancies and document everything. This will be a big key to winning your appeal.
9. Breathe deeply.

[6] M.G.L. c. 59, §§ 11, 38.

State Use Codes:

State Use Code	Road Conditions:	Bldg Style:	Foundation:
013 – Multiuse-Res	P: Paved	BN: Bungalow	PP: Piers Posts
016 – Res-CH61	G: Gravel	RN: Ranch	SL: Slab
017 – Res-CH61A	D: Dirt	RR: Raised Ranch	ST: Stone
018 – Res-CH61B	N: None	SL: Split Level	BK: Brick
021 – Multiuse – OPN		CP: Cape Cod	CB: Concrete Block
031 – Multiuse – COM	Traffic:	RC: Raised Cape	CN: Concrete
061 – CH61-Res	N: None	CL: Colonial	OT: Other
071 – CH61A-Res	L: Light	GR: Garrison	
081 – CH61B –Res	M: Medium	VT: Victorian	Exterior Wall Type:
101 – Single Fam Res	H: Heavy	TD: Tudor	AS: Asphalt Type
102 – Condominium		CN: Contemporary	AB: Asbestos Shingle
103 – Mobile Home	Sewer:	TH: Townhouse	WS: Wood Shingle
104 – Two-Fam Re	SW: Sewer	RE: Row-End	FB: Framed Clapboard
105 – Three-Fam Res	SP: Septic	RM: Row Middle	BK: Brick
106 – Res Land Imp		DX: Duplex	BV: Brick Veneer
109 – Multiple – Residences	Scenic Infl:	DK: Decker	SN: Stone
111 – 4-8 Units	OF: Oceanfront	BL: Bi-Level	SV: Stone Veneer
112 – >8 Units	OV: Ocean View	ST: Stack	CB: Concrete Block
130 – Res Developable Lnd	BF: Bay Front	CO: Conventional	ST: Stucco
131 – Res Part Dvlp Land	BV: Bay View	MH: Mobile Home	MT: Metal
132 – Res Undvlp Lnd	RF: Riverfront	OT: Other	AV: Aluminum/Vinyl Siding
201 – Res Open Land	RV: Riverview		OT: Other
220 – Comm Vacant Land	PF: Pond Front	Roof Type:	
230 – Indus. Vacant Land	PV: Pond View	F: Flat	Heat Type:
300 – Hotel	NO: None	S: Shed	NO: None
301 – Motel		G: Gable	HW: Hot Water
302 – Inn-Resort	Topography:	H: Hip	ER: Electric Radiant
304 – Nursing Home	L: Level	M: Mansard	HP: Heat Pump
305 – Pri-Hospital	G: Gentle Slope	L: Grambrel	OT: Other
310 – Fuel Tank	S: Steep Slope	O: Other	ST: Steam
311 – LP Tank	R: Rolling		SL: Solar
313 – Lumber Yard	W: Underwater	Roofing:	FA: Forced Air
316 – Warehouse		CP: Composition	SH: Space Heat
317 – Farm Bldg		AS: Asphalt Shingle	
318 – Corn Greenhouse		WS: Wood Shingle	
321 – Equip Retail		RR: Roll Roofing	
322 – Dept Store		TL: Tile	
323 – Sh-Cntr/Mall		SC: Slate Clay	
324 – Supermarket		TG: Tar Gravel	
325 – Retail-Store		MT: Metal	
326 – Eating Estbl		OT: Other	
330 – Auto Sales	Fuel Type:	Basement Type:	
331 – Auto Supply	W: Wood	S: Slab	
332 – Auto Repair	O: Oil	P: Partial	
333 – Service Area	E: Electric	X: Full-Exposed	
334 – Gas Station	X: Combination	C: Crawl Space	
335 – Car Wash	N: None	F: Full	
340 – Gen Office	C: Coal	N: None	
341 – Bank	G: Gas		
342 – Med Office	S: Solar	Kitchen/Bath Quality:	
350 – Post Office		L: Luxury	
351 – Educational	Grades/Conditions:	M: Modern	
352 – Day Care Center	E: Excellent	S: Semi-Modern	
355 – Funeral Home	V: Very Good	T: Typical	
380 – Golf Course	G: Good	O: Old-Style	
400 – Manufacturing	A: Average		
401 – Warehouse	F: Fair	Porch/Deck/Etc:	
402 – Office Bldg	P: Poor	S: Screen Porch	
501 – Personal Property	VE: Very Good/Excellent	V: Service	
502 – Corp Property	GV: Good/ Very Good	E: Enclosed Porch	
503 – Manf Property	AG: Average Good	P: Porch	
601 – CH61 – Forest	FA: Fair Average	T: Patio/Slab	
714 – Orchard	PF: Poor Fair	W: Wood Deck	
718 – Pasture	U: Unsound	D: Decorative	

Vision Appraisal Technologies Record Card

We found this format from Vision very straightforward and easy to understand.

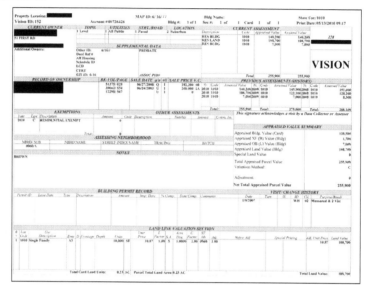

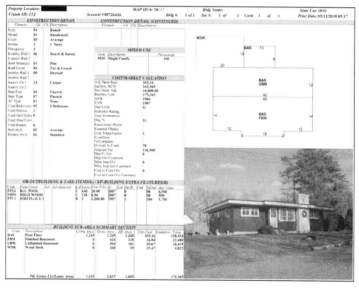

CAMA Record Card

This format is more challenging to decode. Note on this card, you can see that the Market Adjustment entry is blank, yet the increase in value from RCNLD to Cost Building proves that there is some type of Market Adjustment in use. Another curiosity reported to us is that the owner has another home on the property but rather than showing and taxing that home separately, the assessors have combined the square footage of both homes to produce a taxable building cos. This amounts to an unusual tax break for this property owner.

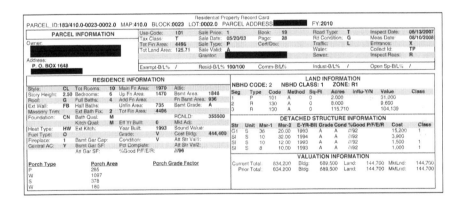

Patriot Record Card

Again, a more challenging format, which generally requires an explanation from the assessor.

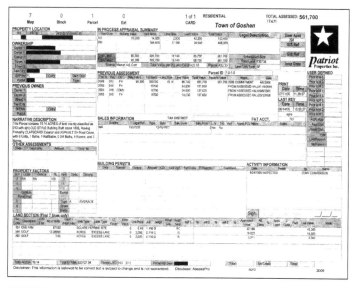

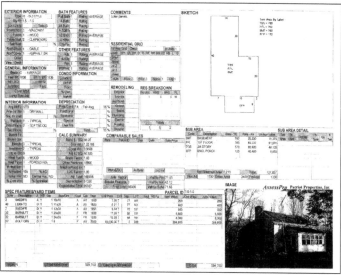

Chapter Six
The Legal Process—Where Do You Begin?

Force always attracts men of low morality. ~ *Albert Einstein*

You now have your property record card and you found mistakes such as the wrong square footage, the wrong number of bathrooms, a non-existent porch or any other mistake regarding your home. For example, my assessor mistook my heating system as air conditioning. Sad, but true. A mistake that incorrectly increased my assessment! Perhaps your neighbor's house, which is just like yours, is assessed much lower than yours, what do you do? The first step is to understand the legal process and how it affects the assessed value of your home.

Although the specific laws differ from state to state, one premise remains the same; you must determine what your house is worth so that you can assess whether you are being properly taxed. In Massachusetts, the assessors are required to assess your home at its "fair cash value" on January 1st of each year.[6] Assessment practices are largely determined by statutory law. Statutory law just means that a state legislature (the people that you vote for) passed laws regarding your property taxes and how to collect them. You must learn the statutory law that is state specific to you. In Massachusetts, the M.G.L. means General Laws and the statutes referred to can be found online at

[6] M.G.L. c. 59, §§ 11, 38.

(The General Laws of Massachusetts). Be advised that these laws can change and it is important to periodically check for the most up to date statutes at the above-listed site. If you do not have access to a computer, you can obtain copies of the statutes at your county law library. The librarian will be of great service to you.

The key to any evaluation of whether to contest your assessment is the answer to the following question: "What is the 'fair cash value' of your home and did the assessors value it too high?" The answer is the holy grail of property tax assessment. The law defines "fair cash value" as the price upon which a willing buyer and a willing seller would agree if both were fully informed and under no compulsion.[7] In other words, use houses sold through "arm's-length" transactions or sales where the buyer and seller have no relationship and the sale is under no duress. Homes that are sold as part of a foreclosure, a "short sale," a divorce settlement, or part of an inheritance are not "arm's-length" transactions. Do not use these kinds of sales in your analysis of the fair cash value of your home. However, if you live in Illinois, a law was just introduced where taxpayers could use foreclosures and short sales in determining the fair market value of their homes. This legislation is still pending and a more in depth discussion can be found in the final chapter of this book.

How do you find out what is the fair market value of your home? Generally, real estate valuation experts, the Massachusetts courts, and the ATB rely upon three approaches to determine the fair cash value of your home: income capitalization, sales comparison, and cost reproduction. The ATB is not required to adopt any particular method of valuation.[8] The sales comparison approach and the cost reproduction will be the two theories that will likely be used to determine the fair market value of your home. The sales comparison method will most likely be utilized

[7] Boston Gas Co. v. Assessors of Boston, 334 Mass. 549, 566 (1956).
[8] Pepsi-Cola Bottling Co. v. Assessors of Boston, 397 Mass. 447, 449 (1986).

by your assessors, but be prepared that some towns and cities utilize the cost reproduction approach. The cost reproduction approach is simply the cost to build the structure minus depreciation.

The law says that sales of comparable properties are strong indicators of fair cash value.[9] You have heard the mantra by many realtors, "location, location, location." So start by finding sales of homes in your area that are like your home for the year preceding January 1st before the fiscal year at issue. Why January 1st? Because the law requires assessors to evaluate the fair market value of your home on January 1st preceding the fiscal year you are contesting. Fiscal years in Massachusetts run from July 1 to June 30th of every year. For example, the valuation date for fiscal year 2010, which runs from July 1, 2009, to June 30, 2010, would be January 1, 2009. Basically, you are looking for homes just like yours that are close to your location and sold in the year before January 1st preceding the year that you are contesting. So, in this example, you would be looking for sales that occurred in 2008. This rule is not written in stone. If you cannot find any comparables, then homes sold after January 1st can be used to prove your home's value, but try to find homes as close to January 1st as possible.

How do you find sales of comparable properties? Those of you who have a realtor friend are in luck. You can access the Multiple Listing Service (MLS) and ask for their analysis of what your home is worth. If you don't have a realtor friend, then try the sites listed at the end of this chapter to give you an idea of what your home is worth. Again, you are looking for comparable sales of similarly situated properties that are sold a year prior to January 1st preceding the year you are contesting. The law calls this type of evidence, "comparable sales" evidence, the best kind to have. The closer the sales are to the location of your home

[9] Foxboro Associates v. Board of Assessors, 385 Mass. 679, 682 (1982).

and the greater the similarity between the sold home and yours, the stronger your case will be. So, you are looking for similar types of properties. For example, if your home is a ranch, then look for ranches. Also look for houses that have similar square footage, land area, number of rooms and other features similar to yours. Bear in mind that the condition of your home and the condition of your comparables are also important. If your home is in excellent shape and you compare your home to another home that has a wrecking crew in the front yard ready to demolish it, your comparable won't do you much good.

Actual sales of the subject property (the home you just bought) are "very strong evidence of fair market value, for they represent what a buyer has been willing to pay a seller for the property."[10] Therefore, if your assessment is based on the purchase price or very close to it, there is not much you can do about it. It gives new meaning to the term, "buyer beware." When you are looking to purchase a home, be prepared to pay property taxes based on the sales price and leave room in your budget to pay these taxes annually.

What if you can't find similar properties recently sold in your area for the year preceding January 1st of the contested tax year? This is a problem that is not usually found in larger towns or cities. However, if you live in a smaller community, then you may face this dilemma. If this is your situation, then try to find comparable sales as close to January 1st as possible. Try to stay within your town, but if sales are non-existent or limited, broaden your search and search in other towns that are located as close to your town as possible. If your property is unique, a geodesic dome for example, you may have to really broaden your search for other similar geodesic homes. Again, the principle remains the same; you are looking for the closest sales to the location

[10] New Boston Garden Corp. V. Assessors of Boston, 383 Mass. 456 469 (1971).

of your home that are as similar to yours as possible.

You can also use the assessed value of comparable properties to prove "fair cash value." This is not an either/or strategy; you can really bolster your case if you bring comparable sales <u>and</u> comparable assessments of similarly situated properties. Using the assessed value of comparable properties in conjunction with comparable sales to prove your case is the best strategy. The strategy remains the same. You want to find similarly situated homes as close to your location as possible.

You can obtain copies of property record cards for comparable properties by going to your assessor's office and requesting them. These records are public records and you are entitled to inspect them.[11] The assessors are required to provide you with copies of the requested public records at reasonable times and without unreasonable delay and must "furnish [a] copy upon payment of a reasonable fee."[12] There is a presumption that the records sought are public records. If the assessors fail to give you the records that you are seeking, then request them in writing and list all of the records that you want. Bring the request down to the assessor's office and have someone in the office give you confirmation that they received your request. It is amazing how many of these requests seem to get lost and never answered. You may also mail the request, but send the letter certified and request a return receipt. It will cost you a few extra bucks, but it is well worth it so that you can prove the assessors received your request. The assessors must respond to this written request in 10 days or they are in violation of the public records law. In your request, you should mention this law and advise the assessors of the 10 day time limit. You should be successful getting your records after this written request. A sample letter is provided at the end of this chapter which contains sample document

[11] M.G.L.c. 66, § 10.
[12] M.G.L. c. 59, §§ 11, 38.

requests that you should be routinely requesting in these kinds of cases.

Additionally, as part of your research, you should also obtain copies of all abatements issued by the assessors to residents for the contested fiscal year and several years prior to the year that you are contesting. What is an abatement? An abatement is a decrease in the assessed value of your home. Abatements are granted when the assessed value of your home is higher than its fair cash value. As part of my research, I uncovered information where assessors' families and friends would often file for and receive abatements, thus lowering their own property taxes. This information will also shed light on whether the assessors are granting abatements for houses similar to yours. This could be added evidence for your arsenal, so request a list of abatements granted and abatements denied as part of your research.

Abatements are a matter of public record and the assessors must give this information to you.[13] However, abatement <u>applications</u> are exempt from public disclosure and you are not entitled to that information. You may encounter the assessors telling you that they do not have to disclose abatement information to you because of the law. Rest assured this is not true. Only abatement applications and supporting information are not public records and therefore exempt from disclosure. The abatement, assessed owner, the fiscal year of the tax, the amount assessed, the amount abated and the date of the abatement is all fair game. If they refuse to give you this information, then follow the procedure above regarding the public records letter.

The more densely populated, techno-savvy towns have assessors' offices that have computerized systems where you can access property record cards directly from a computer that are available for public use. You can access the information by the classification of your home, for

[13] M.G.L. c. 59, § 60.

example, a contemporary home, ranch, etc., and research how other homes like yours are being assessed. Each assessor's office is different, so ask the assessor how to use the computerized system to access the various record cards for similar properties to yours. If your assessor's office is not computerized, ask for a report that lists all of the homes in the same classification as your home so you can find similar homes to yours. If your assessor tells you that they cannot access that information; it is incorrect. Make a formal public records request in writing to the assessors and if they do not respond within 10 days, contact the Public Records Office (for Massachusetts, it's in Boston), and ask them to open a case on the issue.

After obtaining your evidence, you find out that your property is valued in excess of what it should be. What's next? The first step is to file for an abatement. An abatement can be granted by the assessors at the local level or the Appellate Tax Board at the state level. An abatement is your remedy for an over-assessment, or in other words, that an adjustment is required because your assessed value is higher than the fair market value of your home. You can also receive an abatement if you are entitled to an exemption for senior status, are disabled, a veteran, or persons with a temporary financial hardship. Do NOT expect these abatements to be given to you automatically. You still have to file the paperwork to get them. You may also be entitled to an abatement if your home has been improperly classified. Most abatements concerning residential properties are usually based upon overassessments by assessors.

This fact is VERY IMPORTANT.... If you file for an abatement, you must still pay your taxes for the year you are contesting. If you do not pay your taxes and pay them on time, you lose the right to contest your taxes through the abatement procedure.

You begin the process by filing the approved abatement form from the Department of Revenue (DOR). (Check your state link on propertytaxrights.com for your state's forms). A copy of the form can also be obtained from the assessor's office. The City of Boston uses its own form, but the approved DOR form can also be used in Boston. The approved state form does not have to contain detailed information supporting your argument that your assessment is higher than the fair cash value of your home. A simple statement such as "the assessed value of my home is higher than the fair cash value" will be sufficient. You must also check the reasons why you are applying for an abatement. You may apply for an abatement for the following reasons:

1. Overassessment: This box is checked when you believe that the assessors' appraisal of the fair cash value of your home is too high.

2. Disproportionate assessment: This abatement reason requires you to prove that the property is valued at a higher percentage of the fair cash value than other properties due to an intentional, discriminatory assessment policy. This argument is very difficult to prove and usually requires the services of an attorney.

3. Misclassification of real property: The property is misclassified. For example, if the property is classified as commercial and it should be classified as residential. The average homeowner will not likely utilize this reason.

4. Statutory exemptions: You are entitled to an exemption if you are eligible for senior status, are disabled, a veteran or persons with a temporary financial hardship.

You now have your abatement form, should you fill it out and file it at the assessor's office? The answer is "yes." There is no down side to filing an abatement with the assessor's office. It does not cost anything to file. However, there are important filing deadlines that you must comply with or you will lose your right to an abatement. The form must be filed on or before the due date for payment of the first installment of the actual tax bill.[14] Preliminary bills or any notices from the assessors of proposed valuations that assessors send taxpayers during revaluation years do not give you the right to challenge your assessment. Often times your property tax bill will indicate the due date for payment of your taxes and the due date for filing your abatement. Generally, the due date of the application for abatement is February 1st in communities that bill quarterly.[15] In communities that bill twice a year, the due date is 30 days following the mailing of the tax bill.[16] Different time limits apply for the exemptions, so check with your assessor's office for the appropriate deadlines.

The importance of adhering to these deadlines cannot be underestimated. Please be aware that if you miss the deadline, you lose your right to contest your assessment. Moreover, the assessors lose their right to even consider your abatement application (jurisdiction). Even if the assessors want to consider your abatement application, they cannot waive the filing requirements. So, make sure you file your abatement application on time.

Since there is a deadline for filing the abatement form, you should bring the form down to the assessor's office and have someone in the office give you confirmation that they received your abatement application. In order to be legally filed, an application for an abatement must be received by the assessor's office by the close of business on or before the application due date. You may also mail the abatement form, but send the form certified and request a return receipt. You must be

[14] M.G.L.c. 59, § 59.
[15] M.G.L.c.59, §57C.
[16] M.G.L.c. 59, §57.

able to prove that the assessors received your abatement application, otherwise you lose your right to an abatement. In order to be timely filed, the letter must be postmarked by the United States Postal Service as mailed first class, postage prepaid to the proper address of the assessor's office on or before the application due date. Even if the assessors were inclined to give you an abatement, they do not have the power to grant an abatement if you do not file your abatement application on time. Simply put, do not wait until the last moment to file for your abatement. Once the assessors receive the abatement application, they are required to date stamp all applications received and note the delivery method.

You've now filed your application with the assessor's office, now what? The assessors have three months to act on an abatement application.[17] Within these three months, the assessors can do three things: (1) deny the application; (2) grant an abatement, including a partial abatement; or (3) take no action on the application. Usually, the assessors deny the abatement application or fail to take any action. If the assessors fail to act on the application for abatement within three months, the application is "deemed denied" three calendar months (not ninety days) from the date on which the taxpayer filed the application with the assessors. It is very important that you keep track of the dates if you do not hear from the assessors. This is very often a trap for the unwary and could have dire consequences because you will lose your rights to appeal the assessors' decision to the Appellate Tax Board, commonly known as the "ATB." The date for filing with the ATB is discussed in the following chapter.

If the assessors fail to act within three months, your abatement application is therefore deemed denied, the assessors must send you

[17] M.G.L.c. 59, § 64.

written notice of their inaction within ten days after the expiration of the three month period.[18] If the assessors deny your abatement application, they must send written notification within ten days of their decision. This notice, whether through inaction or outright denial, must state the date of the assessors' decision, if any, or the deemed denial date and must state that you have a right to appeal their decision.

Should you negotiate with the assessors? There is no harm in meeting with the assessors to try to solve the differences of opinion regarding the value of your home. If it is resolved, consider yourself supremely blessed. Bear in mind however, that you may want to keep your "ace in the hole" and not show your whole hand to the assessors in case you want to pursue your case further if you feel that the assessors are being unreasonable. Each assessor's office is different and you must evaluate each office on an individual basis. If you resolve your case, you will be in the minority and will have saved money and time litigating the case further. If you do not resolve your case with the assessors, your next step is to pursue your case with the Appellate Tax Board (ATB), which will be discussed in the next chapter.

During the negotiation process, should you allow the assessors to inspect your property or respond to their requests for information regarding your property? The simple answer is "yes." Massachusetts General Law, Chapter 59: Section 38D allows assessors to require property owners to provide, under the pains and penalties of perjury, information which is "reasonably required" to determine the fair cash value of your property.[19] If you ignore their requests and fail to reply, you may forfeit your rights to an appeal at the ATB.

If the assessors request information from you pursuant to Massachusetts General Law, Chapter 59: Section 38D, you must

[18] M.G.L.c. 59, § 63.
[19] M.G.L. c. 59, §38D-38E.

respond in writing within sixty days or request an extension. However, this does not mean that the assessors have free access to your property or can harass you with frivolous requests. The information must be "reasonably required" to determine the fair cash value of your home. If you can prove that the assessors were harassing you or that you were unable to comply with such requests for reasons beyond your control or you attempted to comply in good faith, you will not lose your rights to an appeal with the ATB. Bear in mind however, that the ATB has dismissed cases based upon homeowners' failures to respond to "reasonable" requests for information regarding the fair cash value of their homes. However, failure to respond to the assessors' request for written information from you does not allow the assessors the right to prevent you from filing an abatement application.

You must also allow the assessors an opportunity to inspect your property as well.[20] Furthermore, a taxpayer who chooses to deny the assessors access to his or her property after an appeal is filed with the ATB may face dismissal of the case. In light of this law, if the assessors do come to inspect your property and take measurements, it is a good idea to bring a neutral third party to the inspection as a potential impartial witness. You can bring this witness to your hearing at the ATB if you appeal your abatement denial. In one of my appeals at the ATB, the assessor lied to the ATB commissioner at my hearing and stated that I refused to let the assessors onto my property for inspection. In fact, the assessors had been to my property three times during the contested tax year. Unbelievable you think, but true. Anything is possible, but if you prepare, you can prevent this kind of fraud at your ATB hearing.

With the technology of today, I would also recommend videotaping

[20] M.G.L. c.59, § 61A.

the visit. A taxpayer told me that when the assessors measured the exterior of her home, they measured the length of the exterior walls in a diagonal manner between the two people holding the tape measure instead of the appropriate level horizontal line. As a result of the incorrect measurements, the square footage of the home was wrong. The moral of the story is to document the visit and to be on the safe side, have the assessor sign a statement stating that he or she visited your property on the specified date and the duration of the visit. Simply stated, your strategy throughout the entire abatement process should be "document, document, document." If you cannot resolve your case with the assessors at this stage of the game, you can appeal your abatement denial at the ATB.

STEPS:

1. Make a list of all discrepancies and errors on your property record card.

2. Get all property record cards on all comparable properties.

3. Get all comparable sales of properties for the contested tax year.

4. Get all abatements issued for properties similar to yours.

5. Fill out your abatement form.

6. Send to your assessor via certified mail/return receipt or bring to the assessor's office and have it time stamped and signed.

7. Schedule an appointment with the assessors to review your reasons for requesting an abatement. Determine how much of your evidence to reveal based on how your assessors are likely to handle your request.

8. Mark your calendar for the date by which you should receive an answer from the assessors.

Home Sales & Property Values Websites

Coldwell Banker (website)

No registration necessary! The Coldwell Banker website is a great resource for those looking to sell or buy a home. Homebuyers can conduct property searches, read news articles and watch videos on home buying, obtain neighborhood information and they can also contact a Coldwell real estate professional for guidance. The website also provides sellers with tools to help them estimate the value of their home, research their neighborhood and also help them find a Sales Associate.

CyberHomes (website)

Although an account is not required, signing up for Cyberhomes' free account allows users to view their saved searches from any computer and receive email updates on their saved property searches. The website provides users with a detailed analysis of their home and community. Users can obtain data about property facts, value estimates and up-to-date information about local and national changes in the housing market.

Domania (website)

Domania allows you to conduct easy property searches, find home values for both your home, your neighbor's home and other homes in your area! The site also provides financial

79

information and calculators as well as articles and guides for both sellers and buyers. No registration required!

Eppraisal.com (website)

The website provides home values, neighborhood information, and real estate market analysis. Homeowners, buyers, and sellers can also connect with local real estate professionals, including agents, home inspectors, and appraisers.

HouseFront: Your Real Estate Search and House Value Tool (website)
Home Insight: Property Value & Home Price Check (website)

The website provides you with the week's local market conditions by using their property value and home price checker. The website also provides publications about selling and buying a home, moving, home ownership, home improvement, vacation homes and retirement living. Users can also speak with other homebuyers and sellers in the website's Idea Share Blog.

Home Prices Free (website)

Provides a home comparison service to help homeowners sell their homes. Users will be able to find current market prices of their home by comparing home prices with similar homes that have been recently sold.

RealEstate.com (website)

RealEstate.com provides you with the tools you need to make an informed decision before you buy or sell your home. The website is free to join and allows users to conduct a property search, discover home values, find a loan that is right for them, and also read real estate news articles.

Real Estate ABC (website)

The website provides users with an analysis of market trends, "how to" guides, agent directories and their home values tool. The home values tool gives users an estimated value of the property searched, based on recent home sales.

REMAX (website)

The RE/MAX website allows you to search properties around the world, compare neighborhood home values, read numerous articles in their Learning Center Section and watch videos.

Trulia: Real Estate Search (website)

The website contains up-to-date information on homes for sale, neighborhoods, markets and trends and also helps you find local experts to get advice and your questions answered.

Zillow.com (website)

The website is dedicated to helping homeowners, buyers, sellers, real estate agents, property managers and other real estate professionals find the information they need to learn more about homes, real estate and mortgages. Users can search homes for sale, learn about the latest real estate trends in their neighborhood, homes recently sold, and can also look at possible mortgage solutions. Using the website's real estate directory, user's can locate professionals to ask unanswered questions they may have.

Zip Realty (website)

The site provides a step-by-step guide to help walk visitors through the home selling and buying processes. Visitors can look up homes for sale in their area, find home values, find realtors and many more!

Sample Public Records Request Letter

Date

Town of (name)

Assessors Office

(Address)

To Board of Assessors:

This is a public records request pursuant to M.G.L.c. 66, Section 10.

Please provide me with copies of the following documents within ten days of this request:

1. Any and all Abatements issued for the following years: list years

2. A listing of all residences and addresses in the town of (name) for the following classification (contemporary, ranch, etc.)

3. Property record cards for the following addresses: List the comparable properties that you require.

4. Any and all sales of residences and their addresses in the town for the following years: List years

Please advise me in writing as to any reasonable cost required to fulfill this request.

Thank you for your attention to this matter.

Sincerely,

Name

Address

Chapter Seven
Your Right to an Appeal

Bad laws are the worst sort of tyranny. ~ *Edmund Burke*

You filed for an abatement and it was denied by the assessors. Now what? The specific laws appealing an abatement denial differ from state to state. Although there are similarities concerning the pre-hearing discovery and preparation, you must learn the law that is state specific to you. However, the analysis regarding whether to appeal your abatement denial to the next level will help you no matter what state you live in. Please check the appeal process links that pertain to your state at PropertyTaxRights.com.

In Massachusetts, you can take this to the next step by petitioning the Massachusetts Appellate Tax Board. The Massachusetts Appellate Tax Board commonly referred to as the "ATB" is a quasi-judicial state agency that handles appeals of state and local taxes. The most frequently filed cases at the ATB are real estate tax appeals for both business and private real estate owners.

You have a right to appeal your abatement denial and have a hearing before a commissioner at the ATB. The real question is whether you want to or not. A simple cost/benefit analysis will help you make your decision. In other words, what would it cost you to appeal your abatement denial at the ATB versus what you stand to gain by filing with the ATB. The answer can be found in how big of a mistake the assessors made in your assessment. The larger the mistake, the more money you could save on your taxes. For example, if your assessed value is $100,000 above the fair cash value and your tax rate is 14 per thousand dollars of valuation, then you could save $1,400 for that tax year. An over-valuation of $50,000 would save you $700 in taxes. Remember to consider the tax rate for your town or city when evaluating the assessment error. Since the error rate by assessors across the country regarding the fair cash value of residential homes is over sixty percent, chances are good that you fall into that unfortunate category.

At the ATB, the law is stacked against you. The burden of proof is on you as a taxpayer to prove you deserve an abatement.[21] The assessed value is presumed valid unless the taxpayer meets the burden of proving otherwise. The taxpayer may present evidence of the fair cash value of the property or prove an error in the valuation method.[22]

In other words, you must present evidence of comparable sales or other competent evidence of the fair cash value of your home. Again, "sales of property usually furnish strong evidence of market value."[23] As previously discussed, you should be prepared to bring in evidence of comparable sales and comparable assessments of similarly situated properties. Ideally, a certified appraiser should be hired if the assessor error is large enough to warrant the expenditure. The certified appraiser will form an opinion as to the market value of your home based upon an analysis of sales similar to your residence. The cost of the appraiser will vary according to the complexity of the job. The approximate rate for uncomplicated appraisals for residential homes is

[21] Schlaiker v. Assessors of Great Barrington, 365 Mass. 243, 245 (1974).
[22] General Electric Co. v. Assessors of Lynn, 393 Mass. 591, 600 (1984).
[23] Foxboro Associates v. Board of Assessors of Foxborough, 385 Mass. 679, 682 (1982).

85

around $300. If the error does not warrant this expenditure, then you can proceed without one. Again, comparable sales and comparable assessments are good evidence of the value of your home and can be used at your ATB hearing.

The next consideration in the cost analysis of whether to file with the ATB is the filing fee. The filing fees are based upon the assessed value of your home. If the assessed value is $20,000 or less, the fee is $10. If the assessed value is over $20,000 and equal to or under $100,000, the filing fee is $50. If the assessed value is over $100,000 and equal to or under $999,999, the filing fee is $100. If the assessed value is $1,000,000 or higher, the filing fee is $.10 per $1,000 of the assessed value with a maximum fee of $5,000. In essence, it will cost you a filing fee plus any expert appraiser or attorney you hire. If you decide to represent yourself without a certified appraiser or attorney, it will cost you a filing fee.

As previously discussed, the larger the mistake, the more money you can save on your property taxes. If you convince the ATB commissioner of your position, you will save on all of the taxes you overpaid plus interest. However, based upon personal experience and a review of ATB cases, the commissioners usually do not award the taxpayer a 100% win on his or her case. Typically, the commissioners will usually compromise the positions between the assessors and the homeowner and come somewhere in between the disputed value. A success for the homeowner would be an award of a quarter to a third above what you claim is the true value of your home. Plan on reducing your potential tax savings by a quarter when you are deciding whether the costs versus the potential tax savings make it worth your while to file with the ATB.

Armed with your figures, you can now decide whether to file with the ATB and have a hearing to argue your case. Either the cost/benefit analysis makes it worth your while to file with the ATB, or perhaps the assessors have acted in such an unfair, negligent, corrupt, or retaliatory way, that you decide to file with the ATB on principle alone, regardless of the costs to you. You have two choices in front of you at this stage of the game. You can file under the formal procedure or the informal procedure. Both have advantages and disadvantages.

Under the informal procedure, you must file a petition with the ATB within three months of the date the assessors denied your abatement application. The notice from the assessors has a date of the action on the form. Usually, the form will have two dates on it; the date of mailing and the date the assessors took action. Pay particular attention that you are not looking at the date of mailing. You must find the date of action in the form so that you can correctly identify the date of the assessor's action so you can file with the ATB within the required three months from that date. The same deadline applies to the formal procedure.

If the assessors did not act on your application for an abatement within three months, you must file your appeal within three months from the date the application was deemed denied by law. Reminder: If the assessors failed to act on your application for abatement within three months, the application is "deemed denied" three calendar months (not ninety days) from the date on which the taxpayer filed the application with the assessors. The same deadline applies to the formal procedure.

If you missed the deadline, you can petition (ask) the ATB to extend the time for filing your appeal if you ask within two months after the date the appeal was due.[24] If you are confused about the deadline for filing with the ATB, call the clerk of the ATB (617-727-3100) and ask them for the deadline to file your case. Under no circumstances should you rely on the assessors for giving you the date to file your appeal at the ATB.

Most homeowners file under the informal procedure. This is understandable because most homeowners are not represented by counsel and the unfamiliarity with the process frightens them. However, this may not be the best course of action for most homeowners. The informal procedure eliminates formal discovery and the rules of evidence. Discovery includes, interrogatories (a fancy name for questions), requests to produce documents (asking for letters, property record cards, appraiser reports, etc.), and requests for admissions (agreeing with or denying specific statements). Neither you, nor the assessors, can use any of these discovery mechanisms under the informal procedure. Under the informal procedure, the ATB will serve a copy of your petition on the assessors for you. You also give up your right to appeal to the Massachusetts Court of Appeals, except under very limited circumstances, and you will not be able to ask the ATB for a written explanation of its decision when using the informal procedure.

Another important downside of the informal procedure is that you will not know what the assessors will be arguing or what evidence they will be offering at the ATB hearing. You will not know in advance what comparable sales and comparable assessments the assessors will be presenting at the hearing. As such, you will not be prepared to argue that the sales and assessments used by the assessors are inaccurate indications of market value because the properties differ from yours. In addition, you will be unaware of whether the assessors will be bringing

[24] M.G.L. c. 59, § 65C.

in an appraiser or appraisal report. The upside is that the assessors will not know the evidence that you will be using. You will also not have to spend any time answering discovery requests by the assessors. The decision to proceed under the informal procedure will depend on the strength of your case and whether or not you need to know the assessor's position. If you decide to go this route and your case is within the average homeowner's price range, a lawyer is usually too costly to warrant the expenditure. If you spend money on anything, spend it wisely and obtain the services of a certified appraiser. Again, weigh the cost versus the benefit of hiring one.

If you read the pamphlet issued by the ATB, which can be obtained online at the ATB website, you will find that they provide a lot of information concerning the informal procedure versus the formal procedure. My recommendation is that you proceed with the formal procedure so that you know what the assessors will be arguing at the hearing. The fact that the ATB will be serving your petition instead of you is not a big deal, as you will learn when I teach you how to file and serve the petition for the formal procedure. Moreover, you will probably learn that in most cases, there was very little analysis performed by the assessors in arriving at the assessed value of your home. Surprising, but true. Bottom line, if you have come this far, you are probably willing and capable of putting in the time to proceed with the formal procedure.

However, if you decide to go the informal route, the first step is to file your informal petition at the ATB. You can obtain the form from the ATB website and click on "forms and instructions." An instruction sheet for filling out the form and filing under the informal procedure is also available on the "forms and instructions" tab. Check the "Suggestions for Informal Procedure" tab. Fill out the petition form and send the original and two copies to the ATB (100 Cambridge Street, Suite 200, Boston, MA 02114) with the appropriate filing fee. The check should be made out to the Appellate Tax Board. Make a copy of the petition for your records. The ATB will then serve the petition on the assessors for you. Nothing else is required and the ATB will then send a notice to you of the hearing date. During this time period, if the assessors contact you and want to discuss settlement, entertain their proposals and yes you can settle your case at any time prior to the hearing, at the hearing, or any time prior to the ATB decision. If you come to an agreement, file the appropriate form with the ATB (Agreement as to Fair Cash Value and Decision). Do not, under any circumstances, dismiss your appeal without filing this form. Also, do not take the word of the assessors that they will make the adjustments in your assessment without filing this form with the ATB.

Although most homeowners do not use the formal procedure, there are some important benefits in using this procedure. The main benefit is that you have the right to use discovery to find out what the assessors are doing. You will be able to evaluate the assessors' appraisal methodology and what comparable sales and assessments they utilized in arriving at the assessment of your home. You will have time to prepare your counter arguments and evidence. There is nothing complicated about drafting and responding to discovery. The issue before the ATB commissioner is what is the fair cash value of your home and did the assessors make mistakes in assessing your property. Discovery should always be drafted to address these issues.

You start the formal procedure by filing the "Petition Under Formal Procedure" form, which can be found online (Appellate Tax

Board). Fill out the form and make three copies, one for your file and send the original plus two copies to the ATB (100 Cambridge Street, Suite 200, Boston, MA 02114) with a check for the filing fee made out to the Appellate Tax Board. The clerk will send you back a filed stamped copy for you to serve on the assessor's office. Immediately serve a copy of the filed stamped copy on the assessor's office. Either take the copy to the assessor's office in hand or mail it first class mail with a return receipt requested. If you decide to take the petition personally to the assessor's office, make sure you get proof that you dropped off the petition, i.e. a time/date stamp and signature. Bring another copy of the petition and have someone in the office date stamp your copy that they received it or if no stamp is available, have an assessor sign a piece of paper saying that they received a copy of the petition in hand from you. You will be surprised how some of these petitions get "misplaced."

You then fill out a "Certificate of Service" form, which you can get on line at the site listed above. Make a copy of the certificate of service for your records and send the original back to the ATB for filing. If you served the petition by mail, remember to attach the return receipt from the post office to your certificate of service. If you served it by dropping off the petition at the assessor's office, attach a copy of the proof that you served it in hand to the certificate and mail it to the ATB. Don't forget to make copies of everything for your records. You must file the certificate of service no later than 10 days after you filed your petition. If you miss this 10 day deadline, the ATB can, if they want to, dismiss your case.

After you serve the assessors, the assessors must file an answer with the clerk within thirty days of the date that you served the petition. However, if the assessors raise no issue other than the question whether there has been an overvaluation or improper classification of your home, they do not have to file an answer. If no answer is filed in such a case, the allegation of overvaluation or improper classification of such property shall be held to be denied and all other material facts alleged in the petition admitted. Effectively, since you are probably just contesting the overassessment of your property, you will probably not receive an answer to your petition. Wait about forty days from the date that you served the assessors, then you can begin discovery.

You now have the right to ask the assessors questions (interrogatories) about your case. You should definitely use this tool. As each case is different, you will tailor your questions to getting information about your specific case. However, there are some basic questions that you should ask and a sample form is provided at the end of the chapter. Just add any questions that you might have that you think are important to your case. When you use the formal procedure, read the rules that apply. You can find them on the ATB website under the tab "Rules of Practice and Procedure of the Appellate Tax Board." You can also find these rules at your county law library. These rules are commonly referred to as the Massachusetts Code of Regulations. The regulations for the ATB start at 831 CMR 1.00. These rules will tell you how to file petitions, answers, discovery and motions. Do not be intimidated by the process, you can do this. Just copy the interrogatories provided at the end of this chapter.

With regard to interrogatories or questions, the appropriate 831 CMR rule is under 1.25: Interrogatories to a Party. When you draft these questions, bear in mind that you are limited to thirty questions. That means you count subparts as well. When drafting your questions, don't ask the birthdates of the assessors; make your questions count. So if you get a set of questions from the assessors in excess of the thirty question limit, answer the first thirty, including subparts, and object to the remaining questions because they are over the limit. If a party wants to ask more questions, the party has to ask permission from the ATB in order to do so. That procedure is called a "motion" and I will explain that later on in this chapter. Once you have prepared your questions, file the original with the ATB and serve a copy on the assessors. The assessors must answer your questions within twenty days after they received the questions. They have to file their answers with the ATB and serve you. The answers must be signed by an assessor under oath. You can use the assessor's answers as evidence at your hearing. All of the rules pertaining to interrogatories can be found at <u>M.G.L. c. 231 §§ 61-67 and 831 CMR § 1.25.</u> .

If the assessors have hired an attorney, you will probably get answers to your questions, albeit, most of the questions will not be answered because of some objection or answered in some absurd manner. As an example, this is an actual response from my town's assessors who had retained a lawyer.

> *Question: Please state the methodology utilized to measure and calculate the square footage of the geodesic home. (The assessors could not get the square footage right because the dome was a ten sided structure; it required the utilization of the principles of geometry)*
>
> *Answer: Assessors used a tape measure to obtain the square footage of the building.*

I kid you not, that was the answer submitted by the assessors and signed off by their lawyer. Expect this kind of stonewalling as a matter of routine.

Another common objection is that your question is too burdensome for the assessors to answer or that you are not entitled to the answer for some reason. If the assessors are not represented by counsel, you will probably not get any answers at all. In either case, you can ask the ATB for help in getting your answers. You can file a motion with the ATB and ask that the assessors answer your questions. Even if you do not understand the nature of the objections made by the assessors' attorney, ask for the commissioner to make the assessors answer anyway. There is never any harm in asking. This motion is called a "motion to compel answers to interrogatories" and a sample motion is provided at the end of this chapter. Before you file this motion, call and write the assessors and tell them that their answers are overdue. Keep a copy of the letter because you will be attaching the letter to your motion to compel. You will probably have to file this motion to get the assessors to answer your questions. The answers to your questions can be used by you and your expert, if you hire one, in countering the arguments made by the assessors at your hearing.

You drafted your motion, now what? You call the clerk at the ATB and request a hearing date. Telephone hearings are also available on Mondays at 11:00 a.m. for those of you who live outside Boston. They work just as well as appearing in person at the ATB in Boston. If you are requesting a telephone conference, you must make arrangements for the conference call. The days for motion hearings are listed at <u>831 CMR 1.16</u>. Check the motion dates (usually Mondays) and see what works for you. Pick a date at least several weeks out so that you can serve the assessors or their attorney with the motion. Call the ATB clerk and see if that date is available. The rules state that you cannot serve the motion shorter than seven days before the hearing. Insert the date you picked in your motion. If the assessors call and say that they cannot make the hearing, you can pick a mutually agreeable date, just check with the clerk at the ATB and see if the date is available. If you do not hear from the assessors, then be ready for the motion hearing. Be prepared to tell the commissioner why you want the answers and how it impacts the issue of your home's market value. The commissioner will then issue an order regarding what answers should be answered. The commissioners have been receptive to allowing homeowner's motions to compel assessors to respond to discovery. Remember, do not wait until the last minute to force the assessors to answer your questions, you may need to do more discovery and research, so assert your rights in a timely manner. Don't forget to ask the commissioner for a date that the assessors must respond to your questions.

Another discovery tool is called a "request to produce documents." This is simply a request for documents in the assessor's control such as letters, abatements, property record cards, appraisal reports, reports of all residences within a specific classification of homes, ex. Ranches, contemporary homes, etc., and any other document that you think is important to your case. Once you have prepared your request for documents, file the original with the ATB and serve a copy on the assessors. A sample form is at the end of the chapter. There is no limit to the number of documents you can request from the assessors. If the assessors fail to respond to your request, you can file a "motion to compel documents" and follow the same procedure used in the motion to compel interrogatories. A sample form is provided at the end of the chapter.

Another discovery tool available under the rules is called a "deposition." A deposition is when a witness testifies under oath to questions posed by the opposing side or his or her attorney. This tool is costly and requires more legal skill than the average homeowner is capable of handling. If this tool is utilized, you probably have an attorney and the case involves a business property or a more expensive piece of property. Ignore this section of the rules. See 831 CMR § 1.26.

Discovery tool "Requests for Admissions" are not listed in the ATB rules. However, requests for admissions are authorized by M.G.L. c. 231, § 69 which were made applicable to these kinds of cases by M.G.L.c. 58A, § 8A. "Requests for Admissions" are simply a tool whereby a party asks another party to admit certain facts for purposes of the hearing. If the assessors do not respond within the 10 day deadline, the assessors have admitted the facts as stated in your demand. If the assessors refuse to admit a fact as demanded, the cost of proving the fact may be assessed against the assessors. I have rarely seen this tool utilized in average residential cases at the ATB and it is highly doubtful that you will be awarded costs by the commissioner. Practically speaking, this discovery tool will be of little value to you.

In the formal procedure, if you are served with discovery requests, you should respond to them. With interrogatories (questions), you must type the question out and then your answer. You can object for various evidentiary reasons, but the nature of the law is too extensive to address here. The questions must be pertinent to the issues of your case. If the questions seem intrusive, they probably are and simply answer with the words, "objection, privileged." If the answer would take you years to answer, state "objection, burdensome." A sample "Answer to Interrogatories" is appended at the end of the chapter.

The same objections apply to a request to produce documents. Simply write out the numbered request and if you provide the documents, write "documents attached hereto" and attach the documents to your response. If you want to object, simply write "objection" and the reason for your objection. A sample "Response to a Request for Documents" is appended at the end of the chapter. The assessors will file a motion to compel and let the commissioner decide what you should be required to produce. Bear in mind however, that the ATB can dismiss your case if you do not respond to discovery, so at a minimum, respond to their requests in writing and provide what is "reasonable" and pertinent to the issues of your case.

After you file your petition, whether under the formal or informal procedure, it is taking about a year for the ATB to schedule your hearing. It appears that this wait may be increased due to the backlog generated by many more property owners filing appeals at the ATB.

After you finish getting your information from the assessors, what's next? Should you hire an appraiser? The short answer is "yes" if the cost/benefit analysis warrants it and you have the money. The best evidence will be the appraiser's opinion as to the fair cash value of your home. When you shop for an appraiser, make sure they are certified. A good place to reference is the Appraisal Institute website where you can find certified appraisers from every state in the country. Ask the cost of preparing an appraisal report and what they charge for testifying at your hearing. Depending on where you live, try to get an appraiser who is close to the hearing location so that you can minimize the costs. If you can afford it and the case justifies it, bring an appraiser. You are now ready for the hearing which is explained in the next chapter.

STEPS

1. Decide whether you want to appeal your case to the Appellate Tax Board. Analyze what it would cost you to appeal your abatement denial at the ATB versus what you stand to gain by filing with the ATB. The larger the mistake, the more money you could save on your taxes.

2. Decide whether you want to hire a certified appraiser. This will depend on the size of the assessor error, and what you would save on your taxes versus the cost of the appraiser.

3. Decide whether to file under the formal procedure or the informal procedure.

4. Collect and organize all the data that supports your case.

INFORMAL PROCEDURE

5. File a petition with the ATB within three months of the date the assessors denied your abatement application. Pay the filing fee.

6. Engage in settlement negotiations with your assessors if possible.

7. Wait for the hearing date scheduled by the ATB. The ATB will notify you of the date via the mail.

FORMAL PROCEDURE

8.   File the original petition plus two copies with the ATB with a check for the filing fee made out to the Appellate Tax Board. This petition must be filed within three months of the date the assessors denied your abatement application.

9.   The clerk will send you back a filed stamped copy of the petition for you to serve on the assessor's office. Immediately serve a copy of the filed stamped copy on the assessor's office.

10.   Fill out the "Certificate of Service" form and send the original back to the ATB for filing. File the certificate of service form no later than 10 days after you filed your petition.

11.   Draft your discovery requests (interrogatories and requests to produce documents). Serve them on the assessor's office and file the originals with the ATB with a certificate of service.

12.   If the assessors fail to respond to your discovery requests, draft and file a motion to compel. Serve a copy on the assessors.

13.   Engage in settlement negotiations with your assessors if your case warrants it.

14.   Wait for the scheduled hearing date, which will be set by the ATB who will notify you of the date via the mail.

SAMPLE INTERROGATORIES

COMMONWEALTH OF MASSACHUSSETS
APPELLATE TAX BOARD

DOCKET NO: (PUT # FOUND ON YOUR PETITION)

(NAME OF HOMEOWNER)

Appellant

v.

BOARD OF ASSESSORS OF THE CITY OF (NAME OF CITY)

Appellee

FIRST SET OF INTERROGATORIES OF THE APPELLANT TO BE
ANSWERED UNDER OATH BY THE APPELLEE CITY OF
(NAME OF CITY OR TOWN)

The appellant propounds the following interrogatories to the appellee to be answered under oath within twenty (20) days of this request.

In answering these Interrogatories, the appellee must furnish all requested information, not subject to a valid objection, that is known by, possessed by, or available to him or any of his attorneys, consultants, representatives or other agents.

If the appellee is unable to answer fully any of these interrogatories, he must answer them to the fullest extent possible, specifying the reason(s) for his inability to answer the remainder, and stating whatever information, knowledge, or belief he has concerning the unanswerable portion.

The appellee must supplement his responses to these interrogatories when so requested by the appellant prior to the hearing. In addition, without being requested to do so by the appellant, the appellee must reasonably supplement the answers to all interrogatories requesting the identification of persons expected to be called as expert witnesses at the hearing. Without being requested to do so by the appellant, the appellee must also amend any answer when it is discovered to have been incorrect when made or when it is discovered to be no longer true.

INTERROGATORIES

INTERROGATORY NO. 1:

Please state your opinion, when you formed it, as to the fair cash value of appellant's property located at (give your address). Please break down your opinion of the premises into the fair cash value of the land and the building separately.

INTERROGATORY NO. 2:

Please state each and every reason as to how you arrived at the fair cash value of appellant's property located at (give your address).

INTERROGATORY NO. 3:

Did you use the comparable sales approach in assessing the

value of appellant's property located at (give your address)?

INTERROGATORY NO. 4:

Please state the date, parties, and sales price of all the comparable sales used by the assessors in arriving at the assessment of appellant's property located at (address).

INTERROGATORY NO. 5:

Please state all of the elements of the comparable sales used in assessing the appellant's property which are similar to appellant's property located at (address).

INTERROGATORY NO. 6:

Please state all of the elements of the comparable sales used in assessing the appellant's property that are different from the appellant's property located at (address).

INTERROGATORY NO.7:

Please state all adjustments made by the assessors in addressing any differences between the comparable sales used by the assessors and the appellant's property in arriving at the assessed value.

INTERROGATORY NO. 8:

Please identify and give the owner's names and addresses of all comparable assessments used by the assessors in evaluating the assessed value of appellant's property located at (give address).

INTERROGATORY NO. 9:

Please state all of the elements of the comparable assessments used in assessing the appellant's property which are similar to appellant's property located at (address).

INTERROGATORY NO. 10:

Please state all of the elements of the comparable assessments used in assessing the appellant's property that are different from the appellant's property located at (address).

INTERROGATORY NO. 11:

Please state all adjustments made by the assessors in addressing any differences between the comparable assessments used by the assessors and the appellant's property in arriving at the assessed value.

INTERROGATORY NO. 12:

Please state what computer program the assessors used in generating appellants property record card.

INTERROGATORY NO. 13:

Please state the meaning of all abbreviations for the specific computer program utilized by the assessors in constructing the appellant's property record card.

INTERROGATORY NO. 14:

Please state whether the cost reproduction approach was utilized by the assessors in arriving at their opinion of the appellant's assessed value of the property located at (address).

INTERROGATORY NO. 15:

Please state whether any depreciation was considered and how it was calculated.

INTERROGATORY NO. 16:

With reference to any experts that the appellee expects to call at the hearing:

(a) Please state the name and address and field of expertise of each person whom the appellee expects to call as an expert witness, including any appraisers; and,

(b) Please state fully and in detail the subject matter about which and the substance of the facts and opinions to which each person referred to in your answer to the preceding interrogatory is expected to testify.

INTERROGATORY NO. 17:

ADD ANY OTHER QUESTIONS IN THE SAME FORM THAT YOU THINK ARE IMPORTANT TO YOUR CASE.

By the Appellant
(homeowner's name)

_____

homeowner's name

address

telephone number

CERTIFICATE OF SERVICE

I, (NAME OF HOMEOWNER), do hereby certify that I served a copy of the foregoing First Set of Interrogatories on the appellee City of (NAME OF CITY) by mailing, first class, postage pre-paid, a copy to the Board of Assessors of the City of (NAME) (ADDRESS OF ASSESSORS) on (DATE MAILED THE INTERROGATORIES TO THE ATB).

_____

homeowner's name

SAMPLE MOTION TO COMPEL ANSWERS TO INTERROGATORIES

COMMONWEALTH OF MASSACHUSSETS

APPELLATE TAX BOARD

DOCKET NO: (PUT # FOUND ON YOUR PETITION)

(NAME OF HOMEOWNER)

Appellant

v.

BOARD OF ASSESSORS OF THE CITY OF (NAME OF CITY)

Appellee

MOTION TO COMPEL THE APPELLEE CITY OF (NAME OF CITY) TO ANSWER UNDER OATH THE APPELLANT'S FIRST SET OF INTERROGATORIES

NOW COMES the appellant, (homeowner's name), in the above-mentioned proceeding and hereby moves this court to compel the Board of Assessors of the City of (name) to answer the appellant's first set of interrogatories propounded on (insert date in the certificate of service.)

As grounds therefore, the appellant states and argues the following:

1. The appellant served his first set of interrogatories on

the Board of Assessors of (name) on (insert date.) To date, no answers have been received by the appellant. On (date), I called the assessors and told them that their answers were overdue. On (date), I wrote the assessors and told them in writing that their answers were overdue. See a copy of the letter attached to this motion. I still do not have their answers.

2.   If the assessors have answered your interrogatories, but the answers were inadequate or they simply objected to all or most of your questions, then insert the following paragraph instead of the preceding paragraph where the assessors never answered at all.

The appellant served his first set of interrogatories on the Board of Assessors of (name) on (insert date.) The answers to questions (insert numbers to your questions) are inadequate. The answers to questions (insert numbers to your questions) are improperly objected to.

3.   These answers are essential to the preparation of the appellant's case and the facts sought are admissible at the hearing.

WHEREFORE, the appellant requests that the Board of Assessors of (name of city or town) be compelled to answer the following numbered questions on or before thirty days after the order rendered by the commissioner after hearing on this motion.

By the Appellant
(homeowner's name)

_____

homeowner's name
address
telephone number

NOTICE OF MOTION

Please take notice that the undersigned will bring on for hearing the foregoing Motion on (date) at 10:00 a.m. or as soon thereafter as the parties may be heard.

CERTIFICATE OF SERVICE

I, (name of appellant), do hereby certify that I served the within motion and notice by mailing, first class, postage pre-paid, a copy to the following attorneys of record on (date of mailing) to the following:

Board of Assessors
Address
If represented by counsel

Name and address of counsel

_____

Name of homeowner

SAMPLE ANSWER TO INTERROGATORIES

COMMONWEALTH OF MASSACHUSSETS

APPELLATE TAX BOARD

DOCKET NO: (PUT # FOUND ON YOUR PETITION)

(NAME OF HOMEOWNER)

Appellant

v.

BOARD OF ASSESSORS OF THE CITY OF (NAME OF CITY)

Appellee

APPELLANTS ANSWERS TO INTERROGATORIES PROPOUNDED
BY THE APPELLEE
CITY OF (NAME OF CITY OR TOWN)

The appellant answers the following interrogatories propounded by the appellee:

INTERROGATORY NO. 1:

Type out the whole question here and then answer the question. If you object to a question, simply write out: Objection, burdensome.

Continue with the rest of the questions asked by the assessors.

109

When you are finished, add the following and mail the original to the ATB and mail a copy to the assessors.

I, (name of homeowner) hereby answer, under oath, the foregoing interrogatories propounded by the assessors.

By the Appellant
(homeowner's name)

_____

homeowner's name
address
telephone number

CERTIFICATE OF SERVICE

I, (NAME OF HOMEOWNER), do hereby certify that I served a copy of the foregoing Answers to Interrogatories on the appellee City of (NAME OF CITY) by mailing, first class, postage pre-paid, a copy to the Board of Assessors of the City of (NAME) (ADDRESS OF ASSESSORS) on (DATE MAILED THE ANSWERS TO INTERROGATORIES TO THE ATB).

_____

homeowner's name

SAMPLE REQUEST TO PRODUCE DOCUMENTS

COMMONWEALTH OF MASSACHUSSETS

APPELLATE TAX BOARD

DOCKET NO: (PUT # FOUND ON YOUR PETITION)

(NAME OF HOMEOWNER)

Appellant

v.

BOARD OF ASSESSORS OF THE CITY OF (NAME OF CITY)

Appellee

FIRST REQUEST TO PRODUCE DOCUMENTS OF THE APPELLANT TO BE ANSWERED BY THE APPELLEE CITY OF (NAME OF CITY)

Pursuant to G.L.c. 213, § 68, the appellant requests the Board of Assessors of the City of (Name of City or town) to produce and/or permit him to inspect and copy the documents requested below, on or before 30 days after the date on the Certificate of Service below, or at such other time and place as the parties may agree upon.

First Request:

Please provide all documents of all the comparable sales used by the assessors in arriving at the assessment of appellant's property located at (address).

Second Request:

Please provide all documents of comparable assessments used by the assessors in evaluating the assessed value of appellant's property located at (give address).

Third Request:

Please provide all documents relating to each person expected to be called as an expert witness at the hearing, including but not limited to the following:

a. all documents prepared by each expert witness;

b. all documents relied upon by each expert witness;

c. all documents used, consulted, or reviewed by each expert witness;

d. all documents, including a current curriculum vitae, used to establish each expert's witness's qualifications for purposes of the hearing.

Fourth Request:

Please provide all documents relied upon by the assessors in arriving at the fair cash value of appellant's property located at (give your address).

Fifth Request:

All documents which give the meaning of all abbreviations for the specific computer program utilized by the assessors in constructing the appellant's property record card.

Sixth Request:

All documents identified in your responses to Interrogatories.

(Continue to add additional requests that are specific to your case.)

By the Appellant
(homeowner's name)

_____

homeowner's name
address
telephone number

SAMPLE MOTION TO COMPEL DOCUMENTS

COMMONWEALTH OF MASSACHUSSETS

APPELLATE TAX BOARD

DOCKET NO: (PUT # FOUND ON YOUR PETITION)

(NAME OF HOMEOWNER)

Appellant

v.

BOARD OF ASSESSORS OF THE CITY OF (NAME OF CITY)

Appellee

MOTION TO COMPEL THE APPELLEE CITY OF (NAME OF CITY) TO PRODUCE DOCUMENTS

NOW COMES the appellant, (homeowner's name), in the above-mentioned proceeding and hereby moves this court to compel the Board of Assessors of the City of (name) to produce the documents requested in the appellant's first request for documents propounded on (insert date in the certificate of service.)

As grounds therefore, the appellant states and argues the following:

1.   The appellant served his first request for documents on the Board of Assessors of (name) on (insert date.) To date, no

documents have been received by the appellant. On (date), I called the assessors and told them that their responses were overdue. On (date), I wrote the assessors and told them in writing that their responses and the requested documents were overdue. See a copy of the letter attached to this motion. I still do not have the requested documents.

2.   If the assessors have responded to your request to produce documents and have refused to give you the documents because they simply objected to all or most of your document requests, then insert the following paragraph instead of the preceding paragraph where the assessors never even responded at all.

The appellant served his first request for documents on the Board of Assessors of (name) on (insert date.) The request for documents (insert numbers to your requests) are improperly objected to.

3.   These documents are essential to the preparation of the appellant's case and the documents sought are admissible at the hearing.

WHEREFORE, the appellant requests that the Board of Assessors of (name of city or town) be compelled to produce the documents in the following numbered requests on or before thirty days after the order rendered by the commissioner after hearing on this motion.

By the Appellant
(homeowner's name)

_____

homeowner's name
address
telephone number

NOTICE OF MOTION

Please take notice that the undersigned will bring on for hearing the foregoing Motion on (date) at 10:00 a.m. or as soon thereafter as the parties may be heard.

CERTIFICATE OF SERVICE

I, (name of appellant), do hereby certify that I served the within motion and notice by mailing, first class, postage pre-paid, a copy to the following attorneys of record on (date of mailing) to the following:

Board of Assessors
Address

If represented by counsel
Name and address of counsel

_____

Name of homeowner

SAMPLE ANSWER TO REQUEST TO PRODUCE DOCUMENTS BY THE ASSESSORS

COMMONWEALTH OF MASSACHUSSETS

APPELLATE TAX BOARD

DOCKET NO: (PUT # FOUND ON YOUR PETITION)

(NAME OF HOMEOWNER)

Appellant

v.

BOARD OF ASSESSORS OF THE CITY OF (NAME OF CITY)

Appellee

RESPONSE TO ASSESSORS REQUEST TO PRODUCE DOCUMENTS PROPOUNDED BY THE APPELLEE CITY OF (NAME OF CITY OR TOWN)

Appellant responds to the Assessors request to produce documents as follows:

RESPONSE TO REQUEST #1:

If you are not objecting and are producing the documents, simply write:

Documents are produced and attached hereto.

RESPONSE TO REQUEST #2:

If you are objecting, simply write:

Objection, irrelevant and inadmissible.

Continue to respond to the remainder of the requests.

By the Appellant
(homeowner's name)

_____

homeowner's name
address
telephone number

CERTIFICATE OF SERVICE

I, (NAME OF HOMEOWNER), do hereby certify that I served a copy of the foregoing Responses to appellee City of (NAME OF CITY) Request to Produce documents by mailing, first class, postage pre-paid, a copy to the Board of Assessors of the City of (NAME) (ADDRESS OF ASSESSORS) on (DATE MAILED THE RESPONSES TO THE ATB).

_____

homeowner's name

Chapter Eight
Your Day In Court

There is no such thing as justice—in or out of court.

~ Clarence Darrow

It is the eve of your hearing, is there anything else left to do? You can file a motion with the ATB requesting an exchange of appraisal reports.[25] This motion must be filed at least thirty days before your scheduled hearing date. The strategy concerning whether to file this motion is case specific. There are a myriad of factors that can influence your decision in this regard. Some factors are: whether or not you want to disclose your expert and his report; discovering the assessors' expert and his report; disclosing your expert's and the assessors' expert report to facilitate settlement; and preparing a counter argument and evidence to refute the assessors' expert appraiser. You must evaluate your case to see if you want to exchange reports, but remember the 30 day deadline.

You will be notified by the ATB of the date and time of your hearing.[26] This date can be continued by written agreement of the parties after approval by a commissioner. Hearings before the ATB are

[25] M.G.L.c. 58A, § 8A.
[26] 831 CMR § 1.19.

generally held before a single member of the board. The Board consists of four commissioners and one chairman. The backgrounds of the commissioners vary. Some are attorneys and some are not. All are political appointments of the governor.

You can request that your hearing be stenographically transcribed. You must request an official stenographer at least one day prior to the hearing.[27] Without a stenographic record, neither party can appeal an adverse decision to the Massachusetts Court of Appeals regarding whether certain items of evidence were properly admitted or whether the ATB findings were warranted by the evidence. Filing an appeal with the Massachusetts Court of Appeals is costly and you will probably not want to incur this expense unless the cost/benefit analysis warrants it. In most cases, you will not want to request a stenographer or appeal your case to the Massachusetts Court of Appeals. If you wish to appeal your case to the Court of Appeals, you should retain a lawyer.

The ATB is not required to follow the rules of evidence applicable to the courts of Massachusetts other than the rule regarding privilege.[28] The ATB rules reserve to the board the discretion to relax strict rules of evidence and "to make hearings and proceedings as informal as possible, to the end that substance and not form shall govern."[29]

At the beginning of the hearing, the following documents are usually introduced in order to establish jurisdiction of the ATB:

1.   The abatement application that you filed with the assessors with the date of filing. The original of this document is presented by the Board of Assessors because they have the original.[30]

2.   The tax bill with the date of payment. The original of this document is introduced into evidence by the homeowner. If the original cannot be found, you should get a copy from the tax collector.

---

[27] ATB Rule 1.28.
[28] M.G.L.c. 30A, § 11.

[29] 831 CMR § 1.37.
[30] 831 CMR § 1.22(e).

3. The notice of the decision on the abatement application with the date the notice was given or the fact that no decision was made.[31] Bring this document with you to the hearing.

In practice, these documents will be stipulated (agreed) to be admitted at the hearing without objection. Simply ask the assessors or their attorney if they would agree to admit these documents. If they say "no," don't worry about it, just submit the originals or copies of the preceding listed documents.

Should you make an opening statement? An opening statement is a short synopsis of your case. Ask the board member what his or her preference is. If the board member wants you to give an opening statement, give one. If the board member leaves it up to you, then give one. This is your chance to couch things in the most favorable light to your case. Do not pass up this opportunity to do so. Your opening argument should be brief. Highlight your strongest evidence and stop. Do not dilute your opening by including everything but the kitchen sink. When you are finished with your opening, ask the board member if you may begin the presentation of your case.

What must you prove? As previously discussed, your job is to present "persuasive evidence of overvaluation either by exposing flaws or errors in the assessors' method of valuation, or by introducing affirmative evidence of value which undermines the assessors' valuation."[32] You have the burden to prove your case. This burden shifts to the assessors when the valuation of property has been the subject of an ATB decision for the preceding year and the assessors have raised your evaluation above the ATB assessment. Under General Laws Chapter 58A, Section 12A, the assessors must show that an increase over the ATB's value was warranted. Based upon my personal

[31] 831 CMR § 1.22
[32] Gen. Elec. Co. v. Board of Assessors of Lynn, 393 Mass. 591, 600 (1984).

experience and a review of the ATB decisions, this burden shifting is of very little value to the homeowner and rarely considered by the commissioners when they render their decisions.

You go first, except when there is a prior ATB ruling and the assessors raised your assessment above the prior ATB's ruling. You must evaluate your evidence and decide what to present first. This is ultimately your decision and there is great variation in strategy. It is my practice to put forth the strongest evidence first. As an ex-teacher and well versed in attention spans, I find that most people are attentive in the very beginning of any oral presentation and then their attention quickly dissipates. As such, quickly grab the board member's attention with your strongest evidence.

If you have hired an appraiser, in all likelihood, this will be your first witness. Prepare your questions ahead of time. Nothing is worse than a disorganized direct examination (questioning your own witness) of a witness. A sample direct examination of an appraiser is included at the end of this chapter. Add questions that are specific to your case.

An expert witness, (usually the appraiser) must have special training, knowledge and experience in order to give an expert opinion in a case. You will be asking your own expert about his training and qualifications. In addition, you must keep an eye on whether the assessors' appraiser, if any, is qualified. If they bring in the dog catcher to render a decision on the fair cash value of your property, "object, object, and object." If their expert has sufficient credentials and you know that, obviously do not ask questions concerning his expertise.

At the hearing, the questions you ask your expert will consist of a summary of what's in the appraisal report. You want to elicit the basis for his opinion and then his ultimate conclusion regarding the fair cash value of your home. After you are finished questioning your expert, ask the board member if you can introduce the expert's report into evidence. These reports are routinely admitted into evidence at these hearings unless the expert appraiser is the town's dog catcher.

What if you don't have an expert? Is it a losing battle? No. You can testify to the value of your home. An owner who is familiar with real estate values and with the characteristics of his property and its availability for actual and potential use can properly testify as to its value.[33] Therefore, if you are familiar with your property and have experience dealing with it, you can testify as to its value. Bring a copy of this case with you if the assessors object at the hearing and cite this case to the board member.

If you are using the comparable sales approach, you will be introducing evidence of fair cash value through the introduction of "comparable sales." This methodology is called the market study method or sales comparison approach; the value of similarly situated properties as close to January 1st preceding the contested fiscal year. If you are utilizing the cost reproduction method of valuation, obviously, you will be introducing evidence of cost reproduction. Remember, this method is the cost to build the structure minus depreciation. Your expert, if you have one, will advise you on the most advantageous appraisal method to use. Bear in mind that the sales comparison approach is more commonly used. Remember however, the board is not required to adopt any particular method of valuation.

If you hired an expert, these comparable sales will be contained within the appraisal report. If you did not retain an expert, simply find the appropriate comparables and get certified copies of the sales (deeds) from the registry of deeds in your county. You will introduce these at

[33] Correia v. New Bedford Redev. Auth., 5 Mass. App. Ct. 289, 295 (1977).

your hearing as evidence of comparable sales. Obviously, you will also be introducing the property record cards for these comparables in order to prove their similarity to your own home.

Lastly, you will also be introducing the property record cards of comparable properties to prove fair cash value. At the hearing, you will simply introduce these property record cards. These cards are official public records and are admissible at the hearing. These kinds of records are routinely admitted at these hearings. It has been my experience that board members usually admit disputed documents and evidence and then decide how much weight to give them in rendering their decisions. As such, do not be too concerned in having your evidence rejected.

You presented all of your evidence and witnesses, you now "rest." At this point in time, either the assessors will present their case or they will not present any evidence at all. In an ATB appeal, the assessors are not obligated to put on any evidence if the assessors feel that the taxpayer hasn't produced sufficient evidence to carry its burden of proof of overvaluation. In this situation, the assessors can simply rest their case on the legal presumption that presumes the assessors' valuation is correct.[34] This rarely happens however, so be prepared to counter the assessors' evidence.

If the assessors have retained an appraiser, you have the right to cross-examine (ask questions) him. Be advised that successful cross-examination is even difficult for the most seasoned attorney, so tread lightly. Keep your cross examination short. If you have had the benefit of reviewing his report prior to the hearing because you obtained it through discovery or via a motion, then you should give the report to your expert and have your expert prepare appropriate questions to ask. If you just got handed their expert's report at the hearing, request a

[34] Gen. Elec. Co. v. Board of Assessors of Lynn, 393 Mass. 591, 598-600 (1984).

short recess so that you and your expert can review the document. The commissioners usually allow such requests. After you have reviewed the report, your tactic should be to undermine the expert's qualifications, prove he used the wrong methodology or used comparables that were dissimilar to yours, or that he ignored properties that were identical to yours.

At the hearing, you may be presented with the situation where the assessors or their attorney introduce evidence or exhibits without giving you copies. Customary practice is for both sides to make copies of exhibits for the other side. The normal procedure is to request that you want to introduce an exhibit, you wait for the commissioner's ruling, and if allowed, you hand a copy to the clerk sitting in front of the commissioner, and also hand a copy to the assessors or their attorney. I have experienced more often than not that the assessors do not make copies of exhibits they intend to introduce. If this happens to you, do not sit idly by, request that you be given copies so that you can be prepared and follow the questioning. You will also have copies in case you have to litigate your case the following year. Copies of all exhibits are sent back to the introducing party within 30 days of the ATB's decision.

After the assessors rest, both sides can present closing argument. This is rarely done unless the commissioner requests closing arguments, but don't expect to present one. Trial briefs are allowed, but are not usually utilized in residential cases. However, if the assessors file a trial brief or request to file one at the hearing, you should also file one.[35] Never allow the assessors to have the last word.

The hearing is now concluded and the commissioner will take the case under advisement (will not issue a decision from the bench). The

[35] 831 CMR § 1.30.

ATB has three months from the close of the record to issue its decision in both the formal and informal procedures. The official decision is a one line sentence stating who won, if your home was overvalued and the amount of the abatement, if any. If you want a more detailed explanation for its ruling, you can file a request for Findings of Fact and Report. Either party can request these findings and the request must be made in writing and filed with the ATB within 10 days of the decision date. A copy of this request should be sent to the other party as well. A sample form is provided at the end of this chapter.

What if you lose, should you appeal to the Massachusetts Appeals Court? Probably not. First, in order to appeal to the Appeals Court, you had to request a stenographer to transcribe the hearing, a very costly event. Secondly, the costs to pursue a case at the Appeals Court is prohibitive. It is simpler and more cost effective to simply file for an abatement the following year. Unfortunately, the assessors can also raise your assessment every year as well. It took me five long years to finally end my property tax nightmare. To make matters worse, my nightmare did not end because of my appeals at the ATB, but ended because the assessor corruption in my town was so egregious that adverse publicity forced the assessors to resign or not seek re-election. Aptly said by Clarence Darrow, and true in the case of property tax law, "there is no such thing as justice—in or out of court."

Steps:

1. If you decided that you want to exchange appraisal reports, you must file this motion with the ATB at least thirty days before your scheduled hearing.

2. If you want the opportunity to appeal your case further, you must have your hearing stenographically transcribed. You must request an official stenographer at least one day prior to the hearing.

3. At the beginning of the hearing, introduce your tax bill with the date of payment. Also introduce the notice of the decision on the abatement application with the date the notice was given or the fact that no decision was made.

4. Give an opening statement if the commissioner requests one. Opening arguments are rarely used in these kinds of cases.

5. If you have an expert appraiser, he or she should be your first witness. Introduce the appraiser's report into evidence before he or she leaves the stand.

6. If you did not retain an expert, simply find the appropriate comparable sales and get certified copies of the sales (deeds) from the registry of deeds in your county. Introduce these at your hearing as evidence of comparable sales. Also introduce the property record cards for these comparables in order to prove their similarity to your own home.

7. Introduce property record cards of comparable properties to prove fair cash value of your home.

8. If the assessors have retained an appraiser, cross-examine (ask questions) him.

9. If the commissioner requests a closing argument, then give one. However closing arguments are rarely used in these kinds of cases.

SAMPLE APPRAISER DIRECT EXAMINATION

1. Please state your name for the record?

2. What is your occupation?

3. How long have you been an appraiser?

(Do not ask this question if your appraiser is brand new.)

(Ask about your expert's background here such as special training, member of organizations, experience as a teacher, publications, etc.)

4. Are you licensed?

(If you followed my advice, he or she is.)

5. Have you ever testified in court as an appraiser?

(Don't ask this if they have not)

6. If so, how many times?

7. Were you retained by me to appraise my home?

8. What valuation method did you use to evaluate the fair cash value of my home?

9. Can you explain this method?

10. If your expert used the comparable sales approach, then ask: What comparable sales did you use to arrive at your opinion regarding the fair cash value of my home?

11. Ask for each comparable: How is this comparable similar to my home?

12. Are there any differences in these comparables to my own home? please explain.

13. Did you make any adjustments regarding these differences? please explain.

14. Are your calculations and utilization of these comparables done according to accepted appraisal methodology?

15. If your expert used the "cost reproduction" method, or used this method in addition to a "comparable sales" approach, you should ask the following:

Can you explain the cost reproduction method?

16. Can you describe how you used this method on my home in arriving at your opinion regarding the value of my home?

17. Did you depreciate my home? If yes, then ask, please explain your depreciation of my home.

18. Are your calculations done according to accepted appraisal methodology?

19. Based upon your expertise, do you have an opinion as to the fair cash value of my home?

20. What is it?

21. Did you prepare a report rendering your opinion regarding the value of my home?

22. Show the report to your expert and ask if it is the report he prepared and then ask the board member to have it admitted into evidence.

23. If you have the assessors' opinion and reasons of your home's value in your possession from pre-hearing discovery, then ask your expert why the assessors' opinion of your home's value is wrong. If you are handed an expert report at the hearing by the assessor or his attorney, ask for a recess and have your expert review the report.

Sample questions will include:

Have you had the opportunity to review the assessors' comparable properties in support of their opinion of the value of my home?

Why can't you use this comparable in assessing the fair cash value of my home? Go through the comparables used by the assessor and explain why they can't be used.

What are the differences in the town's comparables that would effect fair market value?

Due to the difference in this comparable to my own home, should an adjustment have been made to incorporate this difference?

Have you had the opportunity to review the assessors' expert's appraisal?

Ask questions regarding why the report is incorrect.

Ask any further questions that are necessary and case specific. Your expert will help you get to the information that is important to the proper evaluation of the market value of your home.

SAMPLE REQUEST FOR FINDINGS
OF FACT AND REPORT

COMMONWEALTH OF MASSACHUSSETS

APPELLATE TAX BOARD

DOCKET NO: (PUT # FOUND ON YOUR PETITION)

(NAME OF HOMEOWNER)

Appellant

v.

BOARD OF ASSESSORS OF THE CITY OF (NAME OF CITY)

Appellee

REQUEST FOR FINDINGS OF FACT AND REPORT

NOW COMES the appellant, (homeowner's name), in the above-mentioned proceeding and hereby moves this court for "Findings of Fact and Report" pursuant to G.L. c. 58A, § 13 and 831 CMR 1.32.

Appellant requests findings of fact and report of the Board's decision issued on (put date in here).

By the Appellant
(homeowner's name)

_____

homeowner's name
address
telephone number

CERTIFICATE OF SERVICE

I, (name of appellant), do hereby certify that I served the within request for findings and report by mailing, first class, postage pre-paid, a copy to the following attorneys of record on (date of mailing) to the following:

Board of Assessors
Address
If represented by counsel
Name and address of counsel

_____

Name of homeowner

Chapter Nine
And The Band Plays On—
Why No State Agency Will Ever Help You

Once Confucius was walking on the mountains
and he came across a woman weeping by a grave.
He asked the woman what her sorrow was, and she replied,
"We are a family of hunters. My father was eaten by a tiger.
My husband was bitten by a tiger and died.
And now my only son!"
"Why don't you move down and live in the valley?
Why do you continue to live up here?" asked Confucius.
And the woman replied, "But sir, there are no tax collectors here!"
Confucius added to his disciples, "You see,
a bad government is more to be feared than tigers."
~ Lin Yutang

Thousands of property owners across this nation are currently embroiled in disputes with their assessors regarding their assessments and high property taxes. Unfortunately, these disputes can drag on for years without any equitable resolution. While preparing for their appeals, many property taxpayers have uncovered unethical and illegal activity on the part of their assessors. Logically, you might ask, "Why don't they report this to their Department of Revenue, their Attorney General, district attorney, or their governmental representatives?" The answer is, they did. They reported their horror stories to all of the above and they did it tenaciously, appropriately and through the proper channels. At the end of this chapter are some of the actual letters sent to the previously enumerated governmental entities. The names and locales are redacted to protect the privacy interests of the concerned individuals and to protect these taxpayers from their well-founded fear of assessor retribution. Predominantly speaking, the governmental response to taxpayers' complaints has been inadequate. Property owners, including former assessors, have called the proper agencies and reported ongoing violations of DOR guidelines and applicable state law. Their telephone calls were followed up with letters, signed petitions and documentation of assessor errors and abuses. These property owners and assessor whistleblowers were treated as if they were annoying flies and their complaints fell upon deaf ears.

Throughout my five year ordeal with my town's assessors, I uncovered systematic negligence and intentional corruption coupled with vindictive practices designed to deter my right to petition my government. Initially, I telephoned the Department of Revenue to voice my concern that I was being targeted for filing a case with the ATB and investigating the practices of the assessor's office. It was self evident that

I was being targeted when the assessors' raised my assessment 47% in the year after I won my case at the ATB. After receiving this ridiculous increase, I immediately offered to sell my house to any assessor for their assessed value of my home. I would have made a handsome profit compared to what it cost to build it. There were no "takers."

Even more suspicious, the assessors issued two property record cards for my property for the same tax year with a disparity of $80,900. There is no rational explanation for the issuance of two property record cards with such a disparity for the same fiscal tax year. I can only surmise that some creative assessment was being performed behind closed doors with regard to my property. Perhaps the assessors picked a number for my total assessed value and then adjusted my record card accordingly? At any rate, something seriously wrong occurred in that office. I reported this to a DOR employee and was told that they had trouble with these assessors before. Why was nothing done about it before I stepped into the quagmire?

My story is not the exception. In 2007, another small town in New England was having serious problems with its assessors. At the request of the selectmen, the DOR investigated the town's Board of Assessors. This is one of the few investigations performed by the DOR. The DOR investigated allegations that property value changes were not uniformly applied and that the changes unfairly benefited the assessors. The DOR found that "the assessors themselves are among the beneficiaries of the changes in valuation."[36] Due to the "questionable practices of one member of the board," an honorable assistant assessor resigned. The corruption was so prevalent that a taxpayer was advised by the assessors in an open meeting to not pay his taxes and let the town take his property. In addition, the assessors failed to follow many of the legal

[36] Town of Ashfield Assessing Department Review Municipal Data Management and Technical Assistance Bureau, June 2007

procedures instituted to ensure fair and equitable taxation in the town. The assessor abuses were often performed behind closed doors because the assessors "were not consistently following the Open Meeting Law."[37] These kinds of stories are indicative of wayward assessing practices that have been reported throughout the country.

In another town, a taxpayer contacted the DOR in order to inform the agency that assessor corruption was so rampant that something had to be done. Joining this taxpayer's voice of concern, other taxpayers telephoned the DOR in an attempt to do "the right thing." In one big voice, these taxpayers told the DOR that the town's assessors were routinely violating the law and many DOR regulations. The complaints alleged that the assessors routinely trespassed onto taxpayers' properties, entered fraudulent numbers on property record cards, refused to carry out revaluations as required by law and assessed their own homes way below market value. Substantiation of these allegations was provided to the department. Indisputable evidence showed that tax bills were not matching the property record cards. This is a very serious problem. The chorus of complaints from concerned citizens elicited a loud retort from a DOR employee, "I will NOT discuss this town anymore." One frustrated taxpayer responded, "So tell me, are we barking up the wrong tree, or are we just barking too loud?" The click on the other end of the phone gave her the answer. This event became another missed opportunity on the part of the DOR to do the right thing and clean up assessor corruption.

Contrary to popular belief, in many states, there is virtually no oversight performed by the DOR of local assessors. Even our political representatives are under the mistaken belief that the department oversees assessor actions. In response to a query from a state senator,

[37] Town of Ashfield Assessing Department Review Municipal Data Management and Technical Assistance Bureau, June 2007

the DOR told the senator's office the following:

"The DOR does not do in-depth investigations as to the assessing practices at the local level as a rule. The Town of ██████, *situation was highly irregular and they do not wish for it to become a precedent. They have informed us that* ██████ *is scheduled for a 2008 certification review by the Department. This occurs every three years, they do an audit of the systems and values used for assessing properties in the town."*

In their own words, in-depth investigations are not the norm. In fact, the DOR is actively fighting making in-depth investigations a "precedent." The extent of oversight by the department is relegated to quick drive bys of assessor selected properties in the town. Further, the alleged three year certification review merely consists of a DOR representative taking several assessor selected record cards in hand and driving by the properties to see if they match up. Obviously, what can be learned about an interior of a home or outbuildings from a several second drive by? The only logical conclusion is that there is essentially no oversight or adequate supervision of assessor practices. This lack of supervision is well-known by assessors and such knowledge is fertile ground for the seeds of corruption to germinate. One assessor who ran her office with an iron hand and her own set of rules stated publicly, "I answer to no one – not even the Attorney General."

Due to DOR inaction to private taxpayers' pleas for help in a town plagued with assessor misconduct, the town's selectmen then asked the DOR for help; they fared no better. The select board repeatedly asked for an investigation to take place; the DOR refused and has not, to this day, provided a thorough investigation of the assessor's office. This letter to a constituent from the town's selectman sums up this town's struggle with getting help from the DOR:

> *"To date, I have had very little confidence in what the DOR has or most likely will do, I only hope that I am wrong....As you probably know, the select board fought a long hard fight to have DOR come and assess what had been repeatedly cited problems in the Assessors' office....but those efforts were thwarted time after time.... we finally felt that ANY involvement by DOR might give us a chance to begin to improve on all financial processes in town....time will tell.....I cannot be too optimistic, but we have got to continue to do the best we can for the town and the townspeople who deserve more than they are currently getting...Again....thanks for the sharing."*

Unfortunately, this selectman was right and the DOR never helped this town. Undeterred by the inertia of the DOR to their plight, these taxpayers sought redress elsewhere. Surely, some governmental agency would get involved? Criminal activity was afoot, albeit white-collar crime. The Attorney General's office is the governmental agency that allegedly oversees the enforcement of criminal statutes. There are criminal statutes pertaining to the "conduct of public officials and employees." These taxpayers decided it was time to contact the Attorney General's Office headed by Martha Coakley. Here is the answer from the Attorney General's office:

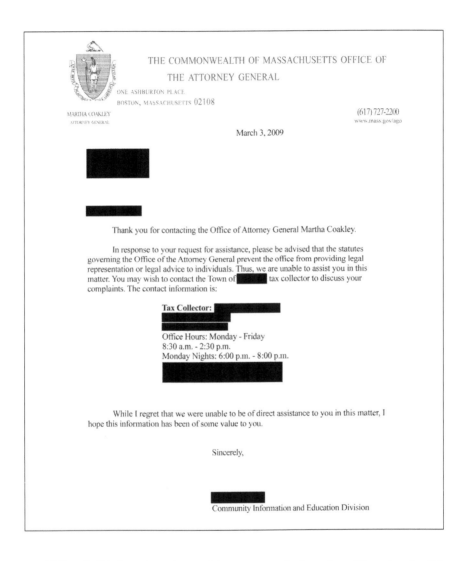

THE COMMONWEALTH OF MASSACHUSETTS OFFICE OF
THE ATTORNEY GENERAL
ONE ASHBURTON PLACE
BOSTON, MASSACHUSETTS 02108

MARTHA COAKLEY
ATTORNEY GENERAL

(617) 727-2200
www.mass.gov/ago

March 3, 2009

Thank you for contacting the Office of Attorney General Martha Coakley.

In response to your request for assistance, please be advised that the statutes governing the Office of the Attorney General prevent the office from providing legal representation or legal advice to individuals. Thus, we are unable to assist you in this matter. You may wish to contact the Town of ▮▮▮▮ tax collector to discuss your complaints. The contact information is:

Tax Collector: ▮▮▮▮▮▮▮

Office Hours: Monday - Friday
8:30 a.m. - 2:30 p.m.
Monday Nights: 6:00 p.m. - 8:00 p.m.

While I regret that we were unable to be of direct assistance to you in this matter, I hope this information has been of some value to you.

Sincerely,

Community Information and Education Division

What is frightening about this response is that the office clearly did not even review the complaint and advised the complainant to pay a visit to a neighboring town's tax collector, an official who clearly has no legal responsibility or power in this instance and who had nothing to do with the complainant's town at all. This bizarre answer from the Attorney General's office prompted this letter from the complainant:

March 16, 2009

Ms. ███████ Community Information & Education Division Office of the Attorney General One Ashburton Place Boston, MA 02108

Dear ███████,

Apparently someone either did not read or did not understand my letter.

Number One:

I was reporting a CRIME committed by PUBLIC OFFICIALS that is occurring in ███████, MA. This is not a personal tax issue, and I wasn't asking for "advice."

Number Two:

This issue is occurring as stated in my letter in ███████ not ███████, MA.

Number Three:

This is clearly not an issue for a Tax Collector in any town.

Will you please get this information to someone else at the Attorney General's Office who handles crimes of tax evasion by public officials? If you have any questions, please call me directly at ███████████ .

Sincerely,

The complainant did not receive another response.
Furthermore, a senator's office contacted the Attorney General's office on behalf of several property owners who asked for a meeting with the AG's office and was told:

> *"The AG's office has informed me that they do not have jurisdiction in this issue. They do not believe a meeting would be helpful."*

A local Attorney General's office further elaborated:

> *"What I can tell you is that there have been discussions on a level above my own with staff attorneys for the DOR. The DOR has taken the position that the present Town of* ███████████ *Assessments issues lies entirely within the DOR's purview at this time. Accordingly, I have been instructed to pass information along to DOR through our Municipal Law Unit."*

It is quite perplexing that DOR attorneys would tell the Attorney General's office not to get involved because they have sole jurisdiction of assessment matters when it is the DOR's specific policy that it does not perform in-depth investigations of allegations of assessor unlawful conduct or abuse of power. At this point in time and in their own words, the Attorney General's office will not handle, address, respond, or enforce crimes perpetrated by any assessor. The DOR will not perform any in-depth investigations concerning assessor malfeasance or unlawful conduct. As such and expressly admitted by the Attorney General and Department of Revenue, assessors are not supervised or held accountable for any of their actions. This lack of oversight and transparency emboldens assessors to do whatever they want with impunity. Trust in state agencies to help bring justice to an insanely unjust property tax system is truly misplaced.

Here is one property owner's e-mail to a senator's office who likened living in her town where the assessors had a "friends & family plan" to living in a third world country where bribes with town officials are an accepted form of business.

"I am at my wits' end here with the Assessor issue. There are 3 assessors on that board and one secretary – all being paid by the taxpayers in a town of only 200 property owners.

As of yesterday, I was informed that they are too busy and can't be bothered printing out the property record cards for 2007. They did not have any problem printing and sending our tax bills which included a change in the tax rate and a revaluation of all property at inconsistent percentages.

Here we are in April and those cards should have been readily available to the public as of January 1, 2007. I have been in touch with the Attorney at Public Records, and he has been most helpful. His office, however, has little enforcement power.

As we continue to be informed, it appears that no one has power over these assessors, and they continue to flagrantly abuse their positions.

The assessors and their friends get low assessments while the people they dislike get high, unsubstantiated assessments. They have publicly threatened people who have questioned what they are doing. One of our neighbors who questioned a $7,000 assessment on a small piece of land he owns was rewarded for his efforts by the assessors then DOUBLING it to $14,000.

As I mentioned to the Senator, the combined abuses amount to terrorism at the local level."

Aptly said. Unfettered power breeds corruption and abuse.

More documented evidence and letters were sent by many residents detailing the constant problems they were having with their assessors. These letters were sent to senators, governors, Attorney Generals, ethics commissions, and District Attorneys across the state. The aggrieved property owners found themselves floating in a sea of total apathy. Their solid evidence was ignored. Property record cards from various towns, to this day, show some of the very same irregularities, mistakes, fraud and vindictive assessments that were shown in black and white to these state agencies years ago. In these instances, the system and its players remain in power in a completely lawless environment. Property owners are still at their mercy.

In one case where a District Attorney's office finally agreed to investigate the Board of Assessors, the property owners' elation quickly turned to despair when they saw the report that was issued. Unbelievably, the investigating officer made the property owners out to be little more than "troublemakers" and simply quoted the assessors' testimony as if it was true despite having documented evidence to the contrary. This bizarre and poor excuse for an "investigation" left the property owners reeling. The investigator had promised a blistering 100 page report on everything from the assessors' mismanagement of records to fraudulent property record entries. Property owners spent hours of their time presenting and explaining the complicated property record cards and mismatched tax bills to the District Attorney's office. I can only imagine the horror the property owners felt when they received a meager 5 page whitewash. These property owners had dared to challenge a corrupt property tax system, which had remained largely hidden for years. One property owner summed it up perfectly, "My mistake was that I thought these agencies wanted to know that the assessors were breaking the law, but they already knew, and they didn't care about anything but covering it up." Given total absolution, assessor irregularities, mistakes, fraud and vindictive assessments continue to this day. And the band plays on!

Bear in mind however, this is not a complete indictment of all assessors. As in any agency, corporation, or association, there are individuals who have an honorable and honest agenda. I applaud these individuals. However, the present property tax system is designed to foster ineptitude and corruption. In Massachusetts, assessors are not required to have a high school degree or any appraisal or assessing experience. In fact, assessors are often elected officials. To make matters worse, assessors in Massachusetts are only required to take a two or three day course and must pass a written, take home exam. That's it. No further training or classes are required. Conceivably, one could be an assessor for twenty years and never increase one's knowledge concerning assessing practices. Ultimately, we have placed the power to assess millions of dollars every year in the hands of people who have very little training or experience. Is it a surprise that the system is not working?

More often than not, I received this response from elected officials and governmental employees: "You have the right to appeal to the Appellate Tax Board." A true statement indeed. However, what the governmental employees, politicians and lay people fail to understand is that the ATB has no enforcement powers, nor are they interested in the practices or corruption of a town's assessors. I, as well as many other complaining taxpayers, were told by ATB commissioners that they are interested in only one thing, "the fair cash value of your property, and nothing more."

Another example of the ATB's lack of enforcement powers that deleteriously effects taxpayers pertains to the interest due homeowners who win their ATB cases. The law requires that interest must be paid to a taxpayer who wins at the ATB for the overpayment of his property taxes at the legal interest rate. For five years, I asked the ATB commissioners for the legal interest owed me because the town refused to reimburse me and I was told that the ATB had no enforcement powers and they could not help me. How is this fair when the government can seize your home when you do not pay your property taxes? How about a law that if the town owes a taxpayer any money for overassessing one's property, then the taxpayer is relieved from paying his or her property taxes until reimbursement with interest is made by the town. With such a law, I suspect that interest and overpayment of taxes will be paid to the homeowner without any delay.

Although the ATB is highly touted as the remedy for overassessment, you can see it is highly overrated. Not only does the ATB not have any ability to enforce its own rulings, the ATB rarely rules 100% in favor of the property owner. ATB commissioners, when they rule in favor of the homeowner, will usually "split the difference" between the assessors' valuation figure and the homeowner's value. For example, let's say you present the value of your home to the ATB as $200,000, and the assessors say the value of your home is $300,000. The ATB rules for you the homeowner, and you "win" your case. It is not unusual, however, for the ATB to set your value at $225,000 or even $250,000 – thus "splitting the difference." This is common knowledge among all professionals who work in this area. So in essence, you never really "win" your case because the commissioners routinely "split the difference." And the band plays on.

Unfortunately, based on statements made by state agency employees, the sad truth is that no state agency will help you. Every avenue was pursued in good faith by concerned property owners across this nation, all to no avail. Said one very discouraged property taxpayer, "We contacted them, and they failed us." All too often these agencies, which are made up of individuals, are more committed to perpetuating their own jobs or the existence of the agency itself rather than the principle that the agency was designed to protect. Namely, the DOR's legal objective is to make sure that real property is assessed fairly and equitably. In the department's own words, "the primary role of the assessors in municipal government is to identify and value all property within a town's boundaries in order to equitably distribute the tax burden." If this is its objective, why is the agency fighting investigative reviews?

The sad reality of the situation is that across this nation there are property owners paying more than their share and those paying less than their share. Regardless of where you fall, any inequity hurts us all. The fact of the matter is that you could be the next unfortunate victim who is hit with a catastrophically high and undeserved property tax bill. It is time for all of us, government employees and private citizens, to do the right thing. If you work for the government, the next time a taxpayer calls with a problem, use the power of the government to help him or her. If you are a citizen, it is your civic duty to join the fight against corruption. It is time for all of us to stand up and be counted.

"We must care for each other more, and tax each other less." ~
Bill Archer

LETTERS

This letter is the DOR's response to multiple property owner complaints.

Massachusetts Department of Revenue *Division of Local Services*
███████, *Commissioner* ███████, *Deputy Commissioner & Director of Municipal Affairs*

September 26, 2007

████████████

Dear Ms. ████

    I have received your letter dated September 21, 2007 regarding a variety of issues concerning the ████████ Assessors. Under current law, the Department of Revenue reviews the overall assessing practices of each city and town once every three years to determine whether they generally result in assessments at fair market value. The Town of ████████ is currently undergoing this certification review.

    Massachusetts' assessors have a constitutional and statutory duty to assess all property annually as of January first at its full and fair cash value. M.G.L. Ch. 59, §§ 2A, 21 and 38: *Town of Sudbury v. Commissioner of Corporations and Taxation,* 366 Mass. 588 (1974). If the assessors believe that prior year's assessed valuations no longer reflect that standard because of changing market conditions, they have a legal duty to reassess accordingly.

    In your letter you allude to a number of concerns some of which I can address in this response to you. Valuation of real and personal property is a complex matter and one that is not always the easiest to understand. You say that fair cash value is determined by arms length sales and is effectuated by equalized assessed valuation ratios (EQV). That is partially correct. Certainly arms length sales are used to aid in determining values but local assessments do not rely on EQVs. EQVs are determined by the Department of Revenue once every two years and are used, i.e., in determining state aid and charges. I refer you to our Guidelines that are available at http://www.mass.gov/Ador/docs/dls/publ/ct/2007/september.pdf. In those guidelines you will find the statistical requirement which note that sale properties must have medians assessment sales ratios between 90 and 110% and coefficients of dispersions ranging from 10% to 20% depending upon the type of property.

    You noted that Chapter 61 calculations are incorrect in many properties. However, the property record cards you sent show that they are being valued as "pasture land" which is the 718 code. I think you must be thinking of the forest land calculations which are 5% of value. I refer you to the Chapter 61A Recommended Farmland Values at http://www.mass.gov/Ador/docs/dls/bla/pdfs/61alval08.pdf. I hope that will help you understand the different valuation methodology.

Post Office Box 9569, Boston, MA 02114-9569, Tel: 617-626-2300; Fax: 617-626-2330

If residents are unable to obtain requested public documents their recourse is to contact the Secretary of the Commonwealth's Public Records Division. Public records enforcement is not within the Department of Revenue's authority.

You refer to the management letter in the audit report for the town. Management letters are written by independent auditor to government officials. They generally identify areas of deficiency, if any, and present recommendations for improvements in accounting procedures, internal controls and other matters. It would be the expectation that local officials would act to correct weaknesses noted by these professional auditors.

In regards to your assumption that properties are under assessed relative to mortgages let me say that the Department neither reviews nor relies on mortgage information. Mortgages are not considered relevant to full and fair cash value of properties and are not part of generally accepted appraisal practices.

A community's proposed property values are reviewed once every three years by the Department. We recommend that assessors maintain a cyclical reinspection program so that all properties are inspected once every nine years, not every three years. We recommend that assessors review sold properties and those with building permits on an annual basis. If assessors were to review all properties once every three years it would be very costly for the community.

As you know, the assessors are required to assess the annual property tax on the fair market value of properties as of each January first. However, property valuation is not an exact science; it involves the application of judgment guided by the use of professionally accepted analytic and appraisal methods. Even with the best of mass appraisal programs, the valuation of some properties may require adjustment. The statutory appeal process, which all taxpayers are eligible to pursue, is designed to enable taxpayers to obtain any appropriate adjustment.

Under current law, the Department of Revenue reviews the overall assessing practices of each city and town once every three years to determine whether they generally result in assessments at fair market value. The Town of ▮▮▮▮▮ is in the midst of its certification review for fiscal year 2008. Your concerns have been noted and are taken seriously. During the certification appraisal staff from the Bureau of Local Assessment will analyze recent property sales and the appraisal methods used by the assessors. The certification review is an audit of the methodology used by the assessors; not a review every parcel in the community. Once preliminary values have been certified by the Bureau the public will have the opportunity to review the proposed values during the public disclosure period before we issue final certification. I urge taxpayers to make every effort to review their proposed values so that any errors can be corrected prior to tax billing.

████████████

Disputes between a landowner and a municipality remain a local issue initially, with the appeal process being to the Appellate Tax Board. In closing, however, we must emphasize that absent agreement with the Board of Assessors as to a value, the exclusive remedy on issues of overvaluation is by appeal to the Appellate Tax Board.

Sincerely yours,

████████████████, Chief
Bureau of Local Assessment

MHB/mhb
Commissioner ██████████
Deputy Commissioner ████████████
███████████, Senior Investigator, Office of the Attorney General
██████████, District Attorney, Northwest District
Senator ████████████

The property taxpayers continue…

October 9, 2007

Ms. ███████████, Chief
Bureau of Local Assessment
PO Box 9569
Boston, MA. 02114-9569

Dear ██████████:

We received your letter dated September 26, 2007 and found your response inadequate for the serious concerns that we have here. You recently investigated ████████ for the same kinds of infractions and revoked that town's certification upon the discovery that only 15% of the assessments were done correctly. ████████ was forced to hire an outside firm - Patriot - and those present assessors resigned.

Now, with assessments corrected and new assessors in place ████████ is following DOR guidelines and the taxpayers are treated fairly and with respect. ████████ wants to be afforded the same fair assessment practices, and asked for your insistence that our Board of Assessor's comply. It is unconscionable that you would allow us to suffer such unfair and illegal practices.

Your representative, ████████ was in our small town for a very short period of time. How would he have any idea what is occurring here unless he conducted a full investigation, re-measured homes and inspected properties? We saw him in town with a few rate cards in hand driving by a few homes. That will never tell the true story of what is happening here. The largest problem is the under assessed and non - assessed properties and clearly those property owners will not be going to Appellate Tax Court. The few, approximately 5 – 10% who are assessed at or near full value are carrying the tax burden for the entire town. This is not in accordance with DOR guidelines.

We are aware that assessors do not use mortgages as a means of assessment, however, a ridiculously low assessment coupled with a high mortgage is a red flag. All of these low valuations are most certainly suspicious and require investigation.

In your response you reference the "public disclosure period" showing proposed property values to ████████ residents. The rate cards that are put out on display by the ████████ Assessor Board, however, have never shown anywhere on the taxpayer's rate card which year they reference. If someone were to go into that office and ask for their 2007 rate card, they would have to take the assessor's "word" as there is no distinction on the cards! Also, the rate cards have not been made available until months after the tax bills have been issued and thus too late for residents to get answers or file abatements for that fiscal year. So the public disclosure period you reference in your letter is of no help to us. Also, do you expect the ████████ Assessor Board to concede or compromise to any of our indications of errors on our supposed rate cards when historically they have refused to answer our questions, provide abatement forms, and provide reasonable public information?

Correspondence and phone calls to and from the Dept. of Public Records takes months and while we are waiting for procedural answers, deadlines are missed and residents are caught unaware that they have then lost all rights to their abatements and property tax adjustments. Basically the assessors' refusal to abide by DOR guidelines has left us with no rights at all.

We are asking for the second time in writing that you thoroughly investigate this town and its assessment practices.

Sincerely,

█████████ &
20 ████████ Residents

Cc: Commissioner ████████ , Department of Revenue
Deputy Commissioner ████████ , Department of Revenue

████████ , Senior Investigator, Office of the Attorney General

████████ , Office of the Hampshire County District Attorney

Senator ████████

Governor Deval Patrick

Another plea for help....

October 16, 2007

Commissioner ███████████
Commonwealth of Massachusetts Department of Revenue
Services
Commissioner's Office
100 Cambridge St.
8th Floor
Boston, MA 02114
Fax: 617-626-2299

Re: Town of ████████ Certification Second Request

Dear Commissioner ███████:

We are formally requesting for the second time that the
Department of Revenue investigate the Town of ████████'s
property assessment procedures. We have proof of the town
assessors' refusal to assess properties accurately and without
bias.

We have proof of vindictive assessments and home visits,
fraudulent entries, incorrect and illegal 61A & B assignments and
calculations, lack of inspections, incorrect measurements, and
just recently the Assessors' refusal to hold a public review for the
residents as required by the DOR.

██████████'s response to our request has offered no solutions and no answers to the illicit assessor activity we continue to be subjected to here in ██████████. After a thorough review of all property rate cards over the last three years we have determined that only a very small percentage of ██████████ properties have been assessed at or near market value. Most of the properties are severely under-assessed including the assessors' own properties and their friends' properties. Thus, only a small percentage of property owners are carrying the tax burden of the entire town.

These under-assessed property owners will certainly not be going to the ATB to get their assessments raised, and the ATB will certainly not lower the assessments of those few properties at or near market value. This unfair burden of taxation will not change without intervention from the DOR.

We need your help and insist that a full investigation be conducted of the assessors' violations of DOR guidelines and also a criminal investigation be conducted of false documents that the assessors have filed.

We have proof of all of this and request again that you revoke ██████████'s certification until both investigations are completed and the assessments have been corrected.

As you are aware, the Commissioner shall enforce all laws relating to the valuation, classification and assessment of property and shall supervise the administration of such laws by local assessors in accordance with the rules, regulations and guidelines established under the law. G.L.c.58 Statute 1A.

At the Select Board meeting held on October 15, 2007, Select Board member ███████ asked Assessor Chair ███████ about the two week public review that is to be conducted in December. ███████ refused to offer this review to ███████ residents. There has never been an annual public review period held in this town conducted by the Board of Assessor's since Mrs. ███████ has been in office, and we are unsure what occurred before her taking this office. We did not know that we should be afforded this, and sincerely doubt that if this were to take place, any contests of assessments would be addressed fairly by this Board.

In closing, there is more than enough evidence to question the professional capabilities of the assessors to properly carry out their public duties. Furthermore, there is more than enough evidence to warrant investigation by the DOR to ascertain whether or not the certification of the town of ███████ should be revoked and criminal charges pressed. Under the law, the Commissioner can cause an assessor to be prosecuted for any violation of law relative to assessment or classification of taxes for which a penalty is imposed. G.L.C. 58 Statute 1A.

We are requesting that this information be forwarded to your investigatory unit of the DOR for investigation of potential violation of the law.

Sincerely,

██████████ &
20 ██████████ , MA. Residents

Cc: Deputy Commissioner ██████████
██████████ / Chief Bureau of Local Assessment
██████████ , Senior Investigator Office of the Attorney General
██████████ , Office of the Hampshire County District
Attorney
Senator ██████████
Governor Deval Patrick

Commissioner ██████████
Commonwealth of Massachusetts Department of Revenue
Services
Commissioner's Office
100 Cambridge St.
8th Floor
Boston, MA 02204
Fax: 617-626-2299
May 23, 2008

157

Another well-written letter from citizens who were simply asking for help from the agency that supposedly oversees assessing practices….

Dear Commissioner ████ ,

We await your response on this very critical issue. As you are aware from past correspondence, we have suffered tremendously at the hands of the assessors here in ████████ over a long period of time. The apparent lack of adherence to DOR regulations and Massachusetts General Law is now legend throughout the state and state agencies.

Our latest very critical problem is that the assessors, although supposedly conducting a formal public disclosure period, as mandated by the DOR, are not available at the hours they themselves have posted. I went to speak with the assessors during their posted hours last night with two other ████████ residents who had questions about their property rate cards. We were informed by ████████ tax collector, ████████ , that the assessors had "assigned" her to be there and answer our questions. The reason that the assessors were not present according to Ms. ████████ , was that "they (the assessors), had a life." Ms. ████████ was unable to answer any of my questions, did not have a key to the assessors' file cabinet, nor access to their computer, could not provide me with a copy of my previous rate card nor provide the new revaluation list as required by the DOR. Ms. ████████ offered to call the assessors and schedule an appointment for the two residents and myself to speak with the assessors directly. It is currently 12:00 on Friday, May 23, 2008, and I have yet to receive a call back with an appointment time. We have also been informed by ██████████ Selectman ██████████'s wife that when she went to speak with the assessors on another evening about her rate card, the assessors were not present and Tax Collector ██████████ answered her questions.

We seriously question the legality of having the town tax collector stand in for the assessors.

We also formally request that the public disclosure period be extended and staffed by the ██████████ Assessors, representatives from the DOR, and from ██████████, and that the reval list be made available for our review.

Sincerely,

██████████

&

██████████ Citizens For Justice

Cc: Attorney General Martha Coakley
Attorney ██████████ / District Attorney's Office
Senator ██████████
Governor Deval Patrick
██████████ Selectboard

A selectboard pleads for help from the Department of Revenue but does not receive it…

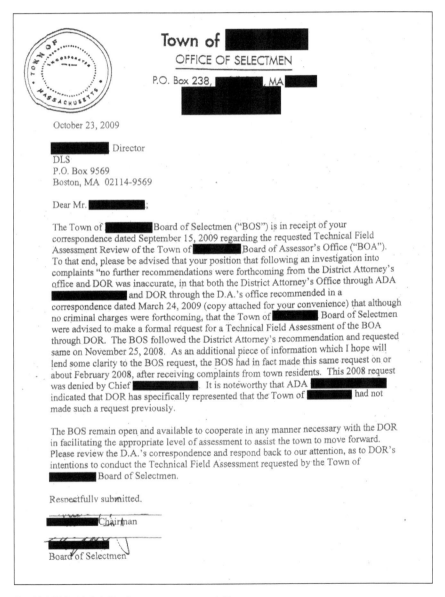

Town of ▮▮▮▮▮▮▮

OFFICE OF SELECTMEN

P.O. Box 238, ▮▮▮▮▮▮▮, MA ▮▮▮▮

October 23, 2009

▮▮▮▮▮▮ Director
DLS
P.O. Box 9569
Boston, MA 02114-9569

Dear Mr. ▮▮▮▮▮▮;

The Town of ▮▮▮▮ Board of Selectmen ("BOS") is in receipt of your correspondence dated September 15, 2009 regarding the requested Technical Field Assessment Review of the Town of ▮▮▮▮ Board of Assessor's Office ("BOA"). To that end, please be advised that your position that following an investigation into complaints "no further recommendations were forthcoming from the District Attorney's office and DOR was inaccurate, in that both the District Attorney's Office through ADA ▮▮▮▮ and DOR through the D.A.'s office recommended in a correspondence dated March 24, 2009 (copy attached for your convenience) that although no criminal charges were forthcoming, that the Town of ▮▮▮▮ Board of Selectmen were advised to make a formal request for a Technical Field Assessment of the BOA through DOR. The BOS followed the District Attorney's recommendation and requested same on November 25, 2008. As an additional piece of information which I hope will lend some clarity to the BOS request, the BOS had in fact made this same request on or about February 2008, after receiving complaints from town residents. This 2008 request was denied by Chief ▮▮▮▮▮▮. It is noteworthy that ADA ▮▮▮▮ indicated that DOR has specifically represented that the Town of ▮▮▮▮ had not made such a request previously.

The BOS remain open and available to cooperate in any manner necessary with the DOR in facilitating the appropriate level of assessment to assist the town to move forward. Please review the D.A.'s correspondence and respond back to our attention, as to DOR's intentions to conduct the Technical Field Assessment requested by the Town of ▮▮▮▮ Board of Selectmen.

Respectfully submitted.

▮▮▮▮ Chairman

▮▮▮▮
Board of Selectmen

Chapter Ten
In Conclusion...

Experience hath shewn,
that even under the best forms of government,
those entrusted with power have, in time, and by slow operations,
perverted it into tyranny. ~ Thomas Jefferson

When I began my journey into property tax hell, I soon discovered that the property tax system was built for corruption and riddled with flaws. After years of battling my town's assessors, negative publicity finally forced them from office. To date, the replacements have followed the law and instituted an open door policy with respect to individual assessments. My ordeal has finally ended. However, like Dante's Inferno, I may be hurled into another layer of hell if there is a change of the guard in the assessor's office. The system has not changed and transparency and accountability are not built into its design. Consequently, a change in assessors always creates an opportunity for graft and abuse. Too much unfettered power is left in the hands of assessors and any potential fairness in taxation is dependent upon the skill and internal moral compass of each individual assessor. Is this the kind of system we want?

Aside from the impossibility of achieving any fairness in the present system, it is time to evaluate the reasoning behind property taxation. The majority of Americans work their entire lives to purchase their homes, the single biggest investment that most Americans will make in their lives. Yet, the reality is, that under the current property tax system, the majority of us are simply renting our property from the government. If you fail to pay your taxes, your property is seized. Property taxes have risen at such an alarming rate that seniors are often driven from their homes or forced to obtain reverse mortgages simply because they cannot afford to pay their property taxes. Is this the legacy that we want for our senior citizens and their heirs? Senior citizens are not the only ones struggling to pay their taxes. The increasing tax burden on the middle class will eventually squeeze it out of existence. Without the middle class, our society resembles a monarchy from feudal times with its great divide between the rich and poor.

Another problem built into the system is that any improvement made to a taxpayer's property increases his or her property tax. This alone should be enough to discard the entire system. Improving one's property and fostering industriousness should be encouraged, not penalized. Did anyone even discuss this negative impact on our communities when this system was instituted?

More importantly, the real problem regarding property taxes is that any system will be unfair and arbitrary. Human frailties such as greed and dishonesty will always undermine any property tax system. The entire system needs to be eradicated because there is truly no way to make it fair. This is not as far out as it may seem. There is a ballot initiative in North Dakota that would amend its constitution to eliminate property taxes altogether. The legislature would have to use state taxes to replace the revenue collected from property taxes and develop a method for distribution. This story is still unfolding. Following the lead in North Dakota, a referendum could be instituted in any state to eliminate property taxes by bypassing your legislature and amending your state's constitution.

In the meantime, you should file for your abatements and do everything in your power to make sure that your assessment is accurate and as fair as possible under the current laws. If you have a group of property owners who were targeted for unfair assessments, join forces and file a class action lawsuit. There is strength in numbers and it will lessen the legal costs.

Dependent upon your state's laws, you can petition your legal representatives to introduce legislation to change the existent laws, which favor the assessors. For example, in Illinois and Georgia, legislation was introduced that would allow foreclosures and short sales to be utilized in determining the fair cash value of homes. The legislation, (in Illinois called the "Property Tax Fair Cash Value Legislation,") will drive assessed property values down and should dramatically lower taxes. It is simply fair that the law should take into account those homes that are in foreclosure and necessarily impact market value. Our link to state petitions for the abolishment of property taxes can be found on our website:

http://PropertyTaxRights.com/

Some states, in order to protect taxpayers from vindictive assessments, will fix a taxpayer's property assessment for a three year period if the homeowner successfully wins his case on appeal. In Massachusetts and other states that do not have this three year rule, a simple legislative change could be passed to fix a taxpayer's property taxes for a three year period if they are successful at the Appellate Tax Board. This simple change alone would prevent retaliatory tax increases by assessors for at least three years. Another obvious legislative action would be to give the Appellate Tax Board enforcement powers to carry out its orders and judgments. Yes, sad but true, the board currently cannot enforce its orders or take any action against assessors who are acting unlawfully. These acts alone would go a long way in leveling out the playing field.

Another creative approach is being used in Maine. Small towns have disincorporated and become unorganized territories. In essence, they have abolished their towns altogether; they simply do not exist anymore. As such, they no longer have to pay for a town government and their property taxes have decreased substantially. Disincorporation may be a possibility for your town if it has 2,000 residents or less. What services are you receiving from your town for the tax dollars you pay? In one small town with 300 property owners and the third highest property tax rate in the state, the total provided services consist of snow removal and road clean up. Is it worth it to have a town status and support a town government if your services are few or nonexistent? This approach has worked in Maine and may be a viable solution for your town's property tax problems.

A referendum or a ballot question is another route to consider if you want to abolish property taxes in your state. A referendum is a direct vote in which an entire electorate is asked to either accept or reject a particular proposal. It is known as a form of direct democracy.

Rules for Referendums in each state can be complicated. They require thousands of verified signatures, adherence to deadlines, and approval by the legislature. This procedure can be very effective, but it is costly and is best left to the professionals. There are referendum experts in every state and you should consult them before going down this path.

If you have uncovered corruption in your town or state, publicize it. Town and state governments are sensitive to negative publicity and it works wonders in getting rid of corrupt officials. Go to your local newspaper, radio and television stations and let everyone know what happened. Then contact your local representatives to get help with your specific case or get them to change the laws. Your representatives will be more receptive if you have the backing of the media. Politicians are acutely aware and sensitive to media exposure.

Lastly, get the word out! Blog about your own situation and the property tax system in general. Use social media, (Facebook, Twitter, etc.) to your advantage. Make use of the forms and petitions at PropertyTaxRights.com. EVERYONE is paying for this unfair system that denies us the right to fully enjoy our homes. Even renters pay for overly burdensome property taxes when their landlords pass them onto their renters by increasing their rent. This unfair taxation has gone on far too long. It is time to speak up, speak out and be a force for positive change!

"All tyranny needs to gain a foothold is for people of good conscience to remain silent." ~ *Thomas Jefferson*

Glossary

Abatement
: An official reduction or elimination of one's assessed valuation after completion of the original assessment. Also, defined as an official reduction or elimination of one's tax liability after completion of the tax roll.

Ad Valorem
: A tax levied in proportion to the value of the thing (s) being taxed. The property tax is an ad valorem tax.

Appeal
: A legal process in which a property owner contests a value or assessment either formally or informally on taxable real or personal property. For each year, there are specific statutory dates when an appeal can be made.

Assessed Value
: The value of property established by taxing authorities on the basis of which the tax rate is applied.

Assessment	The determination as to the value of property that is often used in the levying of property taxes.
Assessment Appeal	A hearing before an Assessment Appeals Board or Hearing Officer where a taxpayer can appeal the amount of the assessed value of his/her property.
Assessment Level	The percentage of full value at which property is assessed as mandated by state law.
Assessor	The elected official whose legal responsibility is to discover, list, classify, and value (appraise) all real and personal property located in his/her jurisdiction.
Classification	The determination of the type of property to be assessed: land, improvements, personal property, fixtures, etc.
Commercial/ Industrial or Business Property	Property used for commercial purposes, i.e., the buying or selling of goods or services, and not for dwelling purposes.
Comparable Sales	Comparable sales are the most common type of evidence used in residential appeals. They represent actual sales of similar types of properties.

Equalization	The process of providing uniform aggregate assessments between townships and counties.
Fair Market Value	It is the price that property would sell for in the open market. It is the price agreed upon by a willing buyer and a willing seller in an "arms length" transaction. The price which a seller of property would receive in an open market by negotiation, as distinguished from a "distress" price on a forced or foreclosure sale, or from an auction.
Improvement	Any structure, addition or other product of labor which is attached, lying upon or within the land that may not be removed without physical stress.
Levy	The amount of money that a taxing body requires to be collected through the property tax system.
Multiplier	A figure used by county and state officials and applied uniformly to all parcels within a township to "equalize" assessments between townships and countries so that all values reflect the same assessment level.

Personal Property	All tangible property except real property (real estate).
Property Tax Appeals Board	A state-level panel of commissioners who review appeals by property owners who are not satisfied with decisions rendered by assessors.
Property Tax	A tax levied on real property for its assessed value which is usually expressed at a uniform rate per thousand of valuation.
Real Estate	Land and anything permanently affixed to the land.
Real Property	Land and anything affixed to the land. Also refers to the interest, benefits, and rights inherent in the ownership of real estate.

About the Author

Patricia Quintilian, Esq. has been practicing law for twenty five years as a trial and appellate attorney. She is licensed in Massachusetts and California and her practice focuses on civil and criminal appellate cases at both the federal and state level. She is also a published legal writer and has been cited in numerous legal publications such as Cornell Law Review, Golden Gate Law Review and Feminist Jurisprudence, Women and the Law by Taylor, Rush and Munro (1999). Many of her cases have been published by the appellate courts. Patricia also taught law students at the collegiate level and presently trains new attorneys in the appellate arena and teaches practicing attorneys at continuing educational seminars.

22127672R00091

Made in the USA
Lexington, KY
13 April 2013